Italian Express

Emily Richards

Italian Express

150 Fast and Easy Family Favorites

For Anne,
Sit back + enjoy
easy cooking.
Mangia bene!
Emily Richards

HarperCollins*Publishers*Ltd

Italian Express

© 2005 by Emily Richards. All rights reserved.

Published by HarperCollins Publishers Ltd

First edition

HarperCollins books may be purchased for educational, business, or sales promotional use through our Special Markets Department.

HarperCollins Publishers Ltd
2 Bloor Street East, 20th Floor
Toronto, Ontario, Canada
M4W 1A8

www.harpercollins.ca

Library and Archives Canada Cataloguing in Publication

Richards, Emily
Italian express : 150 fast and easy family favorites /
Emily Richards. – 1st ed.

Includes index.
ISBN-13: 978-0-00-639514-0
ISBN-10: 0-00-639514-7

1. Cookery, Italian. 2. Quick and easy cookery. I. Title.

TX723.R52 2005   641.5945   C2005-901805-4

RRD 9 8 7 6 5 4 3 2 1

Printed and bound in the United States
Photography: Yvonne Duivenvoorden
Food styling: Claire Stubbs
Prop styling: Maggi Jones
Hair and make-up for cover photo: Jodi Luke
Set in FF Nexus

For my grandparents, who had tradition,
and my parents, who keep it alive.
I love you and I thank you.

acknowledgments

This book was in the making for many years before it came to be. My grandmother, Nana Ortenzia, let me enjoy food when I was young by letting me play with it while I ate it. I think it brought out the best in me.

This last year was busy and full of hard work, but I think it has paid off. Having this book appear has been a dream. I want to thank my friend and mentor, Daphna Rabinovitch, for passing my name to Kirsten Hanson, my editor—this started a great adventure. Kirsten has been so helpful in putting *Italian Express* to pages and helped get more of me into each recipe.

Writing a cookbook, I now know, takes a lot of work, patience and the cooperation of many people. My mom Giustina, dad Tommaso and sister Tina helped in the idea creation, cooking and tasting of all the food. While at home my husband, James, and son Matthew gave me honest truths about the recipes.

My family looked out for me, as I was also pregnant with my second son, Nicolas, during most of the making of this book, and I could only hope that he was another inspiration to cook easy, delicious Italian meals quickly and often. (I can hardly imagine how full my fridge will need to be when Matthew and Nicolas are teenage boys!)

I want to thank HarperCollins Canada for giving me the chance to put my ideas and recipes to paper in a user-friendly book for me to share with all of you. I had many friends and family pass along their favorite easy Italian dinner recipes to include in the book. Thank you to Tom Filippou, Roberto Fracchioni, Michael Mandato, Maria Marotta, Joanne Leese, Zia Peppina and Zia Lina, and all my cousins.

I could not have pushed myself to strive to be as great as my mentors without them. Thank you for inspiring me to become as passionate about food as I am today: Elizabeth Baird, Bonnie Stern, Anne Lindsay, Lucy Waverman, The Canadian Living Test Kitchen and Magazine. Special thanks also to Lesleigh Landry for the nutritional analyses and to Sandra Buffone Maddix for help with the Italian recipe names.

Thanks to the students and viewers of *Canadian Living Cooks* who have come, over the years, to my cooking classes and events across Canada to support my love of cooking and teaching. I hope that you enjoy using *Italian Express* and that you look forward to keeping it in your cookbook collections.

Don't be afraid to go forth into the kitchen and conquer your stoves, pots and pans. Start with a few recipes and then change them up to create your own new ideas and family favorites. Hopefully you can share your stories with me the next time we chat at a cooking class.

Mangia bene sempre.

Con amore,
Emily

contents

foreword

Italian food has been part of my life forever. I was born into a Southern Italian family. My parents grew up in Calabria, a stone's throw away from each other, not knowing that their future would be together in Canada. They each came to Sault Ste. Marie, Ontario, at young ages—my father alone, my mother with her parents.

I know that my name, Emily Richards, doesn't sound very Italian, so I think I should explain it. Emily is my grandmother's name, "Emilia," and Richards is my husband's last name. Even if I'd kept my family name—Fernandes—you'd probably think I was Spanish or Portuguese. But that is a story for another book. Suffice it to say, I'm Italian through and through.

I was born and raised in Sault Ste. Marie. Growing up, I spent a lot of time with my grandmother, mother, aunts, great-aunts and cousins, who all loved to cook. I saw many styles of cooking over the years, and they all influenced my cooking, but it was my mother and grandmother who influenced me most. My grandmother, who stayed at home most of the time, prepared pasta, bread, sauces and meat dishes from scratch, sometimes starting at 4:00 a.m. and cooking all day. When I was very little, she would give me my own pieces of dough with which to create oddly shaped bread and inedible pasta (although, in the end, we always did eat it).

My mother's time, on the other hand, was split between family and work. As a result, she developed the style of cooking I call "Italian express." She could make incredible pasta sauce, but she didn't have a lot of time to prepare dinner when she got home from work. So she took a few shortcuts to create meals that were both quick and delicious enough to serve a hungry daughter and husband.

It is because of these two great influences in my life that I am able to give you *Italian Express,* with its combination of classic flavors and new ideas. With these quick cooking methods, you too can make great Italian food during your weekday rush to feed your family and friends.

Buon Appetito!

introduction

Why Italian Food?

When they say "stick with what you know," it's usually a good idea—and I know Italian! Italian food is beloved because it is a simple, rustic cuisine that most people enjoy. It can be very easy to prepare at home, as many of the ingredients are staples readily available in your pantry. With canned tomatoes, onions, garlic and pasta, a quick and delicious meal is at your fingertips.

On a recent trip back to Italy, I discovered that food is looked at very differently there than it is here. Italians don't buy fast food and eat on the run; they relax and enjoy food and company—especially at lunchtime, or *pranzo*. When *pranzo* rolls around, all the shops and businesses are locked up for the siesta break, and workers go home to spend time with their families and, of course, eat. Italians spend a great deal of time cooking lunch, and even more time eating it. Long-simmered soups and stews, as well as salads, breads and cheeses, make up these lunches, which can be six or eight courses!

Quicker Italian cooking comes into play for *cena*, the evening meal. People who return to work after *pranzo* often come home late and don't want to spend too much time in the kitchen. One or two courses, served at 9:00 or 10:00 p.m., constitutes *cena* for most Italians. I took note of the express-style cooking when I was invited to *cena* at various cousins' homes in Italy, and I've included my favorite recipes here.

In *Italian Express*, you'll find easy, delicious dinner ideas with an Italian influence—not just in their flavors, but often in the way they're prepared as well. Some of the dishes are lighter than others, and you may wish to whip up a salad or some rice to make your meal complete. For heartier dishes, a few slices of crusty Italian bread might be all you need. Many of these dishes make fantastic leftovers, so pack them up for the next day and take them to the office. Lunch never tasted so good!

Spending time in the kitchen can sometimes seem a chore, but it doesn't have to be that way. By keeping core ingredients in your pantry, freezer and refrigerator, you can prepare simple Italian meals every day with little effort. Preparation is key, no matter what type of food you are making. Plan ahead by choosing a couple of recipes before you do your grocery shopping, and you'll be prepared to cook them whenever you like. Your kids can help plan dinner menus too.

Think of the recipes in *Italian Express* as guidelines. If you happen to be missing oregano one night, try a bit of basil instead. Go beyond the recipe to create new flavor combinations. That's the fun of being in the kitchen: being creative and tasting the fruits of your labor.

Food has always been inspirational for me. I love it because it brings so much joy. I hope *Italian Express* inspires you too!

Tips on Equipment

You don't need any special equipment to make great Italian food, but there are a few items that will make your life easier:

- *A sharp chef's knife.* Chef's knives are available in different weights, styles, lengths and prices, and there is one out there that's perfect for you. You must be comfortable with the length and weight of the knife, as you will be using it a lot; if it feels right, you will learn to use it well. I recommend a high-carbon stainless steel knife with a full tang through the handle for strength and stability.
- *A variety of pots and pans.* This will give you the flexibility to cook lots of different dishes. Saucepans have one handle and come in many different sizes; they are perfect for heating sauces or cooking small amounts of food. Pots have two handles and can be deep or shallow. Try to get some with lids (often called Dutch ovens). You'll definitely need a good-size stockpot in which to boil pasta. This can double as a soup pot.
- *Nonstick skillets.* These are easy to clean, and you won't have to use as much oil in your cooking. Take good care of them—if the coating starts to peel or flake off, the particles can get into your food. Buy a new one if that happens. Small skillets are perfect for frying an egg or making omelettes, while bigger ones

are great for frittatas, stir-fries and sauces. If you have a deep skillet, use it to make pasta sauce, and then toss your cooked pasta right in with it.

Many people want to restock their kitchen with new utensils, pots and pans when they decide to do a lot of cooking. I don't blame them—I would like to do that too—but it's not all that realistic. Work with what you have, and gradually add pieces of equipment that you like and need.

Essential Italian Ingredients for Your Pantry

Anchovies

Many people hear the word "anchovy" and run away. But give anchovies a chance: they add richness to any dish you add them to. When cooked in oil, anchovies break down and form a paste that adds a delicious salty flavor to sauces. Anchovy fillets come packed in oil in tins or glass jars. Simply use what you need and refrigerate the rest. (If you use tinned, transfer leftover anchovies to another container.) Anchovies that are packed in salt have a fantastic flavor, but they need to be rinsed before you use them.

You can also buy anchovy paste, which works perfectly anywhere anchovies are called for. It's great for people who don't use anchovies often, as it lasts in the refrigerator for a long time. Look for it in or near the dairy section of your grocery store.

Bread Crumbs

I like to use both dry and fresh bread crumbs. You can find dry bread crumbs in the bakery aisle. There are two kinds: plain and seasoned. The seasoned ones usually have Italian seasonings in them and may be labeled "Italian-seasoned bread crumbs."

To make fresh bread crumbs, pulse bread in the food processor until crumbs form. Make up a batch to keep in the freezer so you will always have them on hand. They are perfect for meatballs, toppings, and as thickeners for some soups. You can use white, whole wheat or even multigrain breads for fresh bread crumbs.

Capers

Capers pack a lot of punch in the flavor department. People often think capers are fish, because they are frequently served with fish, but they are actually the unopened flowers of the caper bush. They are preserved either in vinegar or in salt and have a slightly bitter, almost lemony flavor. They're wonderful for balancing out sweet sauces or for adding a sweet-and-sour taste to a dish. Rinse salt-packed capers before you use them to remove some of the excess salt.

Cheese

What would Italian food be without cheese? Of course, not all Italian food uses cheese, but the two big names when it comes to adding flavor to pasta dishes and soups are Romano and Parmigiano-Reggiano cheese.

Romano cheese is made from sheep's, cow's, or goat's milk and tends to be salty and have a strong bite to it. It is a favorite of the Southern Italians, who don't have many cows wandering their mountains. One famous variety of Romano cheese is pecorino Romano, which is a goat's or sheep's milk cheese. Added to pasta or even a simple omelette, it brightens up the taste considerably. Used mostly as a grated cheese, Romano is also a wonderful addition to pizza, calzones and lasagnas. For an interesting cheese platter, add a wedge of Romano for guests to enjoy while sipping an Italian red wine.

Parmigiano-Reggiano, more commonly known in North America as Parmesan cheese, is a favorite in many households. It has come a long way from its Italian roots and has changed forms somewhat (to that pervasive green container seen on so many kitchen tables). Real Parmigiano-Reggiano is imported from the mother country. It cannot be made anywhere but in Parma, Italy. You can pick it out from a crowd of cheeses because of special markings on the rind that stamp out "Parmigiano-Reggiano," a sign of flavor and distinction. Buying a wedge of Parmigiano-Reggiano to nibble on in chunks or to grate fresh over homemade pasta is a wonderful way to treat your family. You can purchase grated Parmesan cheese made in Canada, which has a somewhat salty flavor. But look out for impostors that don't have to be kept refrigerated, as they don't have all the great taste and melting qualities of the real McCoy. Buy fresh and buy often.

Grana Padano is another hard cheese that can be eaten in chunks or grated on pastas, salads and vegetables. It is richer and less salty than some of the other hard cheeses. I was introduced to this cheese by my father, who is a true cheese lover. I thought he was trying to get a cheap version of Parmesan past me, but in fact he was opening my eyes to the myriad flavors of cheeses. Grana Padano happens to be a little less expensive than Romano or Parmigiano-Reggiano, but that doesn't mean it lacks flavor. It is made with love and care, just as all Italian cheeses are.

I love having all three of these cheeses on hand to enjoy with a glass of wine, sprinkle over pasta or make my cannelloni taste that much more special.

I recommend that you use freshly grated cheese, whether it's Parmigiano-Reggiano or Romano or even Asiago. Buy a wedge or a chunk and use a cheese grater or rasp to grate the cheese—or ask the cheese counter to grate it for you. Many of the available brands of pre-grated cheese have the rind right in them, or are ground to a powder. If you grate your own, the cheese actually melts when you put it on your pasta and has a more delicate flavor than purchased grated cheese. When you're in a rush, buy grated cheese from the deli.

Cured Meats

What exactly are cured meats? Pretty much the best thing since sliced bread! I'm biased, of course, but what can I say? I love the stuff. Meats such as pancetta, prosciutto or soppressata are salt-cured and sometimes contain hot pepper flakes for heat, and pepper sauce or other seasonings for flavor. They are hung to dry, giving them the delicate saltiness and texture that Italians love. They can be eaten raw, but have an intense flavor when cooked, as the salt and spices come to the fore and the texture becomes crisp and brittle—perfect for salads! Look for them in the deli section of your grocery store or head to an Italian deli to try different varieties. There are meats from every region of Italy, and each one is unique and delicious.

Dried Mushrooms

I recommend using dried porcini mushrooms in recipes that call for dried mushrooms. They have a pungent flavor and can be added dried to soups and stews. When adding them to a pasta sauce, it is a good idea to rehydrate them by letting them stand for 15 minutes in boiling water. Remove mushrooms and strain the liquid through a coffee filter to remove any silt, then use it in your sauce. Other dried mushrooms, such as oyster, chanterelle or morel, are also good and can be used in the same way as porcini. The dried versions of these mushrooms tend to be much less expensive than fresh, but usually have tons more flavor.

Garlic

There is no substitute for fresh garlic, chopped when you need it. I like to peel a bunch of garlic cloves and keep them refrigerated in an airtight container. When I need garlic, it's ready to go. Use a sharp knife to chop or mince garlic instead of squishing it through a press. This will preserve all the essential oils that give garlic its great flavor—you want all that deliciousness to go in your food, not onto the press! The best part about garlic is that it gets sweeter as it cooks, and oh, so tasty.

Hot Pepper Flakes

To add some heat and lots of flavor, I use hot pepper flakes (also known as dried chili flakes or red pepper flakes). These are little red chili peppers that have been dried and pulverized to make flakes. You can add them at the beginning of or during the preparation of a dish, or right before you serve it. My dad loves a good heavy sprinkle on his pasta before he starts eating, so it became a popular condiment in our house. Hot pepper flakes add heat, but also a slight sweetness. I sometimes use them instead of black pepper for a true Italian flavor. Purchase hot pepper flakes in bulk so you'll always have lots to go around. For a quick meal, try using them to spice up olive oil, then toss in some cooked shrimp or pasta.

Italian Herb Seasoning

You can purchase Italian herb seasoning at the grocery store in jars or bags. It is a heady mixture of dried herbs that gives dishes tons of flavor. I use it so much that I created my own mixture (see recipe, page 17). You can make a big batch and share it with friends or keep it all for yourself. Be sure to use it within six months or the herbs will start to lose their flavor.

Italian Parsley

I love to use Italian parsley, also known as flat-leaf parsley, both in cooking and for garnish. It has a clean flavor and works very well in all types of cooking, not just Italian. I find it doesn't stick in your teeth as much as curly parsley!

Olive Oil

There are many uses for, and varieties of, olive oil. I use extra-virgin olive oil, which has a rich flavor. Many countries produce olive oil, and each country's oil has a different flavor. I tend to use Southern Italian–style olive oils, which are full-bodied and richly fatty. I also enjoy Northern Italian–style olive oils, which have a fruity and peppery bite. It's all about personal preference. Sample different olive oils and pick the one you enjoy best. You don't need different kinds for different uses, and you don't have to break the bank. Simply buy one in your price range that tastes good and drizzle it over meats, add it to tomato sauce or use it for sautéing or for dressing salads.

If a strong olive flavor is not what you're looking for, try an olive oil with less flavor, such as regular or virgin olive oil, or just use vegetable oil. Vegetable oil works best for deep-frying or when large quantities of oil are needed.

Store oil in a cool, dark place (not under your sink, please, as the pipes make it too warm). For longer storage, keep it in the refrigerator, but try to use it up within its "best before" lifespan, which can be up to two years. If you do keep oil in the refrigerator, you will need to let it come to room temperature before using it, as it tends to solidify slightly when cold. Whether you keep it in the cupboard or in the fridge, the flavor will change slightly over time, so use it up as best you can—cooking Italian food will help!

Pasta

Dried

Short pasta comes in boxes or bags, with a little hole for you to peek in and see the shape of the pasta—it's hard to remember all those Italian names! Short pasta can work with both white sauces and red sauces, and often works best with a chunky or meaty sauce. Tubular types such as penne rigate and rigatoni can hold a lot of sauce. Any short pasta that says *"rigate"* has ridges in it to help sauce stick. But don't shy away from the *"lisce"* or smooth pastas, as they have solid sticking power as well. It's fun to try out new shapes such as Scoobi Doo pasta (cavatappi), wagon wheels (rotelle) or bowties (farfalle). When your kids are shopping with you, let them pick out a bag or two; it might get them to eat more and encourage them to help out in the kitchen.

Long pasta is simply that. I don't know many people who don't have a box or bag of spaghetti in the pantry, crying out for some pasta sauce and meatballs. But there is more to long pasta than spaghetti. Linguine ("little tongues") and fettuccine ("little slices") are becoming more common as more people try new sauces with their pasta dishes. One of my favorite long pastas is bucatini ("little holes"), which has a hole through the center of its long length. It's great for slurping up the sauce that gets caught in it. But if you don't like messes, you can do what my mom does: politely cut up your pasta and eat it with a spoon. Whether you like to cut it, twirl it, slurp it or pick it up with your fingers and drop it in your mouth, the varieties of long pasta are endless. When you try fusilli lunghi, you may even forget about your beloved spaghetti!

There are so many varieties of tiny pasta shapes that soup pasta, or pastina ("little pasta"), really is a category on its own. There are stelline ("little stars"), farfallini ("little bowties"), rounds, squares and even alphabet shapes. Babies love it, and many Italians have childhood memories of devouring bowlfuls of pastina made for us with loving care (and, of course, homemade stock) by our nanas. When I am feeling blue, cooking up some soup pasta always puts a smile on my face. Traditionally used in stews and in soups such as minestrone or chicken noodle, pastina is also a wonderful addition to your side dish repertoire. Try tossing cooked pastina with vegetables and adding a splash of oil and vinegar.

Fresh

You can make your own pasta when you have time, but who has time during the week? Not I! So purchase fresh pasta for a super speedy weeknight meal. Admittedly, the cost is a little higher, but the convenience might be worth it: fresh pasta takes just 3 to 5 minutes to cook. The variety available has increased over the years, and you can now get both long and short fresh pasta—fettuccine, linguine, spaghetti, penne and rigatoni, to name a few. Fresh pasta tends to be lighter in flavor and texture than dried pasta, mainly because of the eggs used to make it. It tastes fresh, because that's what it is. Dried pasta is a firmer-textured pasta made from durum wheat, and it can taste heavy and hearty compared to fresh.

Pasta Sauce

It would be best if we could always make our own pasta sauce, but there often just isn't enough time in the day. Luckily, many companies have provided us with a variety of canned and jarred pasta sauces. Try different brands and see which you like best. Whether it is sun-dried tomato, tomato and basil or four cheese, there's one for every taste. Look for pasta sauce that has tomatoes as the first ingredient.

Once opened, be sure to use up your pasta sauce within a day or two. Use chunky-style sauce to bulk up a spaghetti dish or as a pizza sauce. Add sautéed ground meat to a jar of sauce for a quick meal even the kids will enjoy. A couple of tablespoons (25 mL) will add flavor to your stir-fries, soups and rice dishes and can turn a side dish of peas into a singing sensation.

When you have time, whip up a batch of Homemade Pasta Sauce (see recipe, page 20) and keep it in the fridge or freezer to add true Italian flavor to your cooking.

Pesto

Pesto is a versatile sauce used widely in Italian homes. You can toss it with pasta or add it to vinaigrette for a salad (one of my favorite things to do), and it's great on pizza. Add it to soups, stews and pasta sauces for depth and tons of flavor. You used to have to make pesto yourself in peak basil season, but now you can get it in tubs or jars at the grocery store. If you do grow your own basil, of course, you should make your own pesto (page 18), freezing it for later use.

Traditional pesto is a brilliant combination of flavors, incorporating basil, cheese, garlic, pine nuts and olive oil. But there are other varieties of pesto available too, such as roasted red pepper pesto, sun-dried tomato pesto and various herb combinations. Look for tubs in the fresh pasta section of the grocery store, where they are kept refrigerated. This type of pesto tends to have the best color and flavor and the freshest ingredients. The jarred variety tends to be a bit darker in color and stronger in flavor. Look for pesto that has basil as the first ingredient. If garlic is the first ingredient, make sure you are ready for the flavor to bite back at you.

Rice

Many varieties of rice are used in Italian cooking. There are three that can be used for risotto alone! Try them all and see which you prefer. Arborio is usually the easiest to find in stores, but if you want something with a little more bite in the center, look for Carnaroli or Vialone Nano rice. These are a bit more expensive, but are of higher quality. All three are short-grain varieties that can be used in soups or stews as well as risottos. Because they are high in starch, they add that comforting, creamy consistency to risotto as the outer starch layer cooks away. They keep extremely well and are perfect pantry staples.

Salt and Pepper

Seasoning food is up to you; it just depends on your taste. I have added salt and pepper to many of the recipes in this book, but you can leave them out or add as much or as little as you see fit. My measurements are just guidelines—feel free to experiment and discover what you like best.

I use a few different kinds of salt in my cooking. When I was in Italy, I used sea salt. I also like kosher salt, which is slightly coarse and has no iodine added. Most people use table salt, which has been iodized, and that is what I used when testing these recipes. But I have also made many of them with sea or kosher salt with great success, so it's up to you whether to go with the old standby or try a new one.

When it comes to pepper, on the other hand, I use freshly ground every time. The ready-ground pepper can be quite hot, adding more heat than flavor. Pepper should add some spice, but not too much. Oddly enough, Italians don't use much black pepper, preferring the flavor of hot pepper flakes.

Stock

Many stocks are used in Italian cooking, including beef, vegetable and fish stocks. But chicken stock is certainly the most important. You can make your own; as everyone says, "It's so easy to make stock." Using roasted chicken makes the flavor of the stock deeper and richer, and you can add leeks, onions, garlic, carrots, celery, black peppercorns, thyme and … well, the list is endless. Filling a pot with water and chicken and letting it simmer away can really make your house a home.

No one ever says no to homemade chicken noodle soup, do they? Of course not, especially if they happen to be sick with a cold or flu. That said, there is much more you can make with stock than just soup. It makes wonderful sauces, stews and roasted dishes because it adds flavor without adding fat. Chicken stock can be used with fish, vegetables, pork, veal and, in some cases, turkey or other poultry. It's mild enough not to take over a dish, but it adds more flavor than water.

Beef stock is best when used with beef, but I love adding it to veal, pork and lamb dishes as well to deepen the flavor. Vegetable stock can replace chicken stock in pretty much any recipe. Fish stock, while used sparsely in Italian cooking, is still important as an addition to fish-based risottos and pastas to emphasize the fish flavor.

What should you buy if you can't make your own stock? There are so many options:

Tetra Paks Just shake and pour into a soup or stew, and you have a quick and easy meal. Always the perfect thing for deglazing a pan.

Cans A concentrated stock that can be diluted with equal parts water, or more if it tastes too salty. You can also purchase low-sodium versions.

Pastes A concentrated stock that must be diluted with water. Keep some in the fridge so you can whip up stock any time.

Cubes A concentrated stock that you dilute in hot water. There are many brands, and you must choose wisely. Experiment to see which gives the most homemade flavor without being too salty. And check the ingredients to see how much natural flavor is added. When you see little green things floating around, it's safe to say dehydrated parsley was used, which always helps the homemade flavor come through!

Sun-dried Tomatoes

I prefer sun-dried tomatoes packed in oil. They have a deep tomato flavor, and I like using the oil in my salad dressings. You can purchase them julienned for a quick addition to pasta sauces or salads. If you buy dry-packed sun-dried tomatoes, you will need to rehydrate them in boiling water (or, for more flavor, in vegetable or chicken stock). You can then use the liquid in whatever you are making.

Tomatoes

Not everyone has the option of canning their own tomatoes each summer and storing hundreds of jars. (Maybe I should start selling mine!) But the canned tomatoes you buy at the grocery store are very high quality plum tomatoes that have been picked in season, at the peak of freshness. Finding the brand you like best will take some trial and error. First, taste a couple of brands raw, then cook them in a tomato sauce and see which one gives the best flavor. You shouldn't need to add sugar or baking soda to help with acidity; with cooking, the natural sweetness comes out of the tomatoes.

Canned tomatoes come whole, diced, crushed and stewed—no matter what you're cooking, there is an option out there for you. For quick cooking, I recommend diced tomatoes. They are great for chunky sauces and stews. You can purée whole tomatoes to make wonderful sauces, or break them up and add them to stewed dishes for a true rustic feel. Crushed tomatoes usually include some tomato paste, which makes them a bit sweeter. Stewed tomatoes already have some seasoning in them, such as onions, peppers and garlic, and are great for adding a quick flavor boost to sautés.

Tomato paste is also very useful. It makes sauces thicker and adds sweetness. Because it is so concentrated, a tablespoon or two (15 or 25 mL) gives a great deal of flavor.

Tips for Cooking Pasta

- Some pasta sauces are so quick to make that the sauce will be ready before the pasta, so as a rule of thumb always put your water on to boil first.
- Use a nice big soup pot or stockpot to boil pasta. I add salt to the water once it comes to a boil, before I add the pasta.
- When you add the pasta, give it a good stir so it doesn't stick together or to the pot. Some people suggest putting oil in the water to prevent sticking and overboiling, but if you watch the pot and stir every now and then you won't have any trouble.
- Each pasta has a different cooking time based on its shape, size and texture. Taste it to see if it's done. You are tasting for an al dente texture, which means "to the tooth." The pasta should offer a bit of resistance when you bite into it, and you'll be able to see some white inside. If you prefer softer pasta, by all means keep cooking it until it is done the way you like it.
- Drain pasta in a colander and give it a shake or two before adding it to the sauce. The only time you should rinse pasta is if you are making a pasta salad, or if you are making lasagna and the noodles need to sit a bit before you assemble the dish. Use cool water in this case.

essential recipes

Here are some basic recipes you will find useful when preparing the meals in this book. I whip many of these up on the weekend to use throughout the week. Not to worry: if you're short on time, you can use store-bought in a pinch.

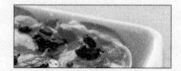

Homemade Pizza Dough

Makes 1 lb (500 g) dough, enough for one 14-inch (35 cm) pizza

This dough can be used to make a traditional thin crust that is perfect for pizzas, and it also makes terrific bread and buns.

Note

If freezing or refrigerating overnight, place dough in oiled resealable bag instead of a bowl. Refrigerate for up to 2 days or freeze for up to 2 weeks. Let thaw in fridge overnight. Let both come to room temperature before using.

Pinch granulated sugar
2/3 cup (150 mL) warm water
2¼ tsp (11 mL) active dry yeast

2 tbsp (25 mL) extra-virgin olive oil
¼ tsp (1 mL) salt
1½ cups (375 mL) all-purpose flour

In a large bowl, dissolve sugar in water. Sprinkle with yeast and let stand for about 10 minutes or until frothy. Whisk in oil and salt. Stir in flour. Scrape out onto a floured work surface and knead until dough forms. Cover and let rest for 30 minutes. Knead again on floured surface until smooth dough forms. Place in a greased bowl, cover with plastic wrap and let stand for about 1 hour or until doubled in bulk.

per 4 oz (125 g) dough 240 calories, 6 g protein, 8 g fat, 37 g carbohydrates, 2 g fiber

Emily's Italian Herb Seasoning Mix

2 tbsp (25 mL) dried oregano
2 tbsp (25 mL) dried basil
1 tbsp (15 mL) dried thyme

1 tbsp (15 mL) crumbled dried sage
2 tsp (10 mL) dried rosemary,
  crumbled
½ tsp (2 mL) hot pepper flakes

Makes about ⅓ cup (75 mL)

A great gift for anyone who loves to cook, this combination of herbs is delicious on chicken, fish and veal, or tossed into a pasta sauce for a burst of flavor. Make batches to send out to family and friends.

In a small bowl, combine oregano, basil, thyme, sage, rosemary and hot pepper flakes. Pour into a spice jar and seal. (*Store at room temperature for up to 6 months.*)

per 1 tsp (5 mL) serving 5 calories, 0.5 g protein, 0 g fat, 1 g carbohydrates, 1 g fiber

Basil Pesto

Makes about 1½ cups (375 mL)

Make pesto in the summer and freeze it for year-round use. Make a few batches so you'll have enough to last all year. If you do run out, basil is now usually available year-round in grocery stores.

2 cups (500 mL) packed fresh basil leaves
¾ cup (175 mL) freshly grated Parmigiano-Reggiano cheese
¼ cup (50 mL) pine nuts

2 cloves garlic, minced
¼ tsp (1 mL) salt
Pinch freshly ground black pepper
¾ cup (175 mL) extra-virgin olive oil (approx)

In a food processor, pulse basil, cheese, pine nuts, garlic, salt and pepper. With machine running, slowly drizzle in oil until smooth. *(Scrape into an airtight container and refrigerate for up to 3 days or freeze for up to 6 months.)*

per 1 tbsp (15 mL) serving 90 calories, 2 g protein, 9 g fat, 1 g carbohydrates, 0 g fiber

Roasted Garlic

1 head garlic
1 tbsp (15 mL) extra-virgin olive oil

Preheat oven to 400°F (200°C). Cut off top of garlic head to expose cloves. Drizzle with oil and place cut side down on a piece of aluminum foil. Wrap and roast for 30 to 40 minutes or until soft when squeezed. Let cool slightly and squeeze out garlic.

Tip

Roast a baking sheet full of garlic heads. Let cool and place in airtight freezer bags or containers and freeze for up to 1 month. Let come to room temperature before using or warm them in the microwave to soften.

Roasted Garlic Aioli

1 head roasted garlic (see recipe, above)

1 cup (250 mL) mayonnaise

Squeeze garlic into a bowl and mash with a fork. Add mayonnaise and stir to blend. *(Cover and refrigerate for up to 2 days.)*

Makes 1 cup (250 mL)

This garlicky mayonnaise makes a sweet and delicious spread for hamburgers and sandwiches—or try dipping roasted potatoes into it.

Per 1 tbsp (15 mL) serving 100 calories, 0 g protein, 11 g fat, 1 g carbohydrates, 0 g fiber

Homemade Pasta Sauce

Makes about 4 cups (1 L)

This is an easy sauce to make on the weekend for use through the week. It's great with pasta or with meats. The halved onion and whole garlic cloves add a more subtle flavor to the sauce than chopped onions and garlic would. With cooking they become very soft and tasty, but you can remove them before serving if you prefer.

2 cans (each 28 oz/796 mL) tomatoes
8 sprigs fresh Italian parsley
4 leaves fresh basil
2 cloves garlic
1 onion, halved

¼ cup (50 mL) extra-virgin olive oil
1 tbsp (15 mL) dried oregano
1 tsp (5 mL) salt
½ tsp (2 mL) hot pepper flakes

In a blender or food processor, purée tomatoes until smooth; pour into a large saucepan. Add parsley, basil, garlic, onion, oil, oregano, salt and hot pepper flakes; bring to a boil. Reduce heat, cover partially and simmer, stirring occasionally, for about 2 hours or until thickened. Remove onion and garlic, if desired. (*Store in airtight container in refrigerator for up to 5 days or in freezer for up to 3 weeks.*)

Per ½ cup (125 mL) serving 120 calories, 2 g protein, 7 g fat, 11 g carbohydrates, 3 g fiber

Spinach Ricotta Gnocchi

1 pkg (10 oz/300 g) fresh baby spinach
2 eggs
1 tub (16 oz/454 g) ricotta cheese

3 cups (750 mL) all-purpose flour
 (approx)
½ tsp (2 mL) salt

Makes about 2 lbs (1 kg), enough for 4 to 6 main course servings

Rinse spinach and place in a skillet over medium heat. Cover and steam in the water that clings to the leaves for about 3 minutes or until wilted. Drain and refresh under cold water. Squeeze with your hands until spinach is dry, then chop and set aside.

In a large bowl, whisk together eggs, ricotta and spinach. With a wooden spoon, stir in 2½ cups (625 mL) of the flour, ½ cup (125 mL) at a time, and salt until soft dough forms. Transfer to a floured work surface and knead in remaining flour as needed for about 5 minutes until smooth dough forms.

My dad's sister, Zia Lina, makes these delicate little dumplings for special occasions and even for family meals. If you're not a fan of spinach, just omit it.

Divide dough into 8 pieces; roll one piece at a time into a long thin strand, about ½ inch (1 cm) in diameter. Cut each strand into about twenty-four 1-inch (2.5 cm) pieces.

Tip
Fresh gnocchi—firmed up for 2 hours in freezer—will take about 3 to 4 minutes to cook.

Roll each piece across the tines of a fork or gnocchi paddle. Place in a single layer on a floured baking sheet. Repeat with remaining dough. Place in freezer for about 2 hours or until firm. Once firm, transfer to a freezer bag. Freeze for up to 6 months.

To Cook
In a large pot of boiling salted water, cook frozen gnocchi for 5 to 7 minutes or until they float to the top and are tender throughout. Remove with a slotted spoon and toss with sauce.

Per each of 6 servings 400 calories, 20 g protein, 12 g fat, 53 g carbohydrates, 3 g fiber

Chicken Stock

Makes about 6 cups (1.5 L) stock and about 3 cups (750 mL) shredded meat

When you make your own chicken stock, you can control the amount of salt you add. Chicken stock freezes perfectly, so make lots and keep it frozen until you need it.

Tips

When the stock first comes to a boil, skim off the top foamy layer for the first 15 minutes.

You can also refrigerate the stock overnight, then remove the fat that forms on top of the stock.

To cook stock in a slow cooker, add all the ingredients to slow cooker and cook on low heat for 8 to 10 hours. Follow directions in recipe for straining.

1 chicken (about 3 lbs/1.5 kg), cut into pieces
2 unpeeled onions, quartered
2 carrots, halved
2 stalks celery, halved
6 cloves garlic
4 sprigs fresh Italian parsley
2 bay leaves
1 tbsp (15 mL) black peppercorns
1 tsp (5 mL) dried thyme
8 cups (2 L) water
Salt (optional)

In a large stockpot, combine chicken, onions, carrots, celery, garlic, parsley, bay leaves, peppercorns and thyme. Pour in water and bring to a boil. Reduce heat, and simmer for 2 to 3 hours or until meat begins to fall off the bone.

Remove chicken to a large plate and let cool. Strain stock through a fine-meshed sieve or a colander lined with cheesecloth. Skim fat from stock. Remove meat from bones and reserve meat for another use or chop and add to stock for soup.

Add salt to taste, if desired. *(Transfer stock to an airtight container and refrigerate for up to 3 days or freeze for up to 6 months.)*

VARIATIONS

Vegetable Stock: Omit the chicken and add 2 leeks, white and light green parts only, coarsely chopped. Place leeks, onions, carrots, celery and garlic on a baking sheet lined with parchment paper and roast in 400°F (200°C) oven for about 40 minutes or until golden. Transfer to a stockpot and add 6 cups (1.5 L) water, parsley, bay leaves, peppercorns and thyme; bring to a boil. Reduce heat, and simmer for about 1 hour or until vegetables are very soft and stock is golden in color. Follow directions above for straining. Add salt to taste.

Fish Stock: Decrease water to 6 cups (1.5 L). Omit chicken and add 3 lbs (1.5 kg) whitefish bones, skins and heads (gills removed) and 1 cup (250 mL) dry white wine. Bring to simmer and simmer for 15 minutes, skimming foam. Follow directions above for straining.

Roasted Chicken Stock: Place chicken pieces, onion, carrots, celery and garlic on large parchment paper–lined baking sheet and roast in 400°F (200°C) oven for about 40 minutes or until chicken is no longer pink inside and vegetables are golden. Scrape into large stockpot and continue with recipe.

Tip

You can also add shrimp, crab or lobster shells with the fish bones.

Per 1 cup (250 mL) stock 35 calories, 2 g protein, 0.5 g fat, 6 g carbohydrates, 1 g fiber

soup

Soups make a kitchen the true heart of the home. They are comforting, and can be thick and hearty or smooth and silky. In Italy, soups tend to be rustic and rich in flavor and texture. When I make soup, I want the aromas to be intoxicating enough to entice my family to the table. That's why I love cooking: the senses are engaged even before you sit down to eat.

Many people think of soups as winter warm-me-ups, but they are great year-round. Some of the soups in this chapter are thick and stew-like—perfect after a long day of skiing—but the lighter soups, such as Stracciatella Soup (page 27), are great with a salad on a summer evening. These recipes are easy to prepare and have a robust taste that will keep you coming back for more.

Golden Soup

Zuppa Dorata

Makes 2 to 3 servings

This soup gets its golden color from the saffron threads, which are used throughout Italy to provide a slight lemony flavor and a gorgeous orange hue.

Tips

Sprinkle with freshly grated Parmigiano-Reggiano before serving.

Try using other thin soup noodles, such as fedelini tagliati.

6 cups (1.5 L) vegetable or chicken stock (store-bought or see recipe, page 22)
1 tsp (5 mL) saffron threads
1 tbsp (15 mL) butter
4 oz (125 g) angel hair pasta

2 eggs
½ cup (125 mL) whipping (35%) cream
2 tbsp (25 mL) chopped fresh Italian parsley

In a large saucepan, bring stock and saffron to a boil. Reduce heat to a simmer. Add butter and stir until melted.

Meanwhile, break pasta into 1-inch (2.5 cm) pieces. Add to stock and simmer, stirring occasionally, for about 5 minutes or until al dente (tender but firm to the bite).

In a small bowl, whisk together eggs, cream and parsley. Gently pour into stock, stirring constantly, and simmer, stirring, for about 4 minutes or until egg is set and stock is thickened.

Per each of 3 servings 440 calories, 20 g protein, 25 g fat, 34 g carbohydrates, 2 g fiber

Stracciatella Soup

Zuppa Stracciatella

6 cups (1.5 L) chicken stock (store-bought or see recipe, page 22)
4 eggs
⅓ cup (75 mL) freshly grated Parmigiano-Reggiano cheese

3 tbsp (45 mL) chopped fresh Italian parsley
Pinch freshly ground black pepper
Pinch freshly grated nutmeg

Makes 4 to 6 servings

This soup is perfect when you have nothing but eggs in the fridge. *Stracci* means "little rags," which is what the egg mixture forms when stirred into the stock. The parsley adds color and flavor.

In a large saucepan, bring stock to a boil. Reduce heat to a simmer.

Meanwhile, in a small bowl, using a fork, beat together eggs, cheese, parsley, pepper and nutmeg. Slowly drizzle into stock, stirring constantly, and simmer, stirring constantly, for about 3 minutes or until egg is set.

VARIATIONS

If you happen to have some spinach in the crisper, add about 1 cup (250 mL) thinly shredded spinach to this soup. A chopped red bell pepper would be delicious, too.

For a different twist, substitute pecorino Romano cheese for the Parmigiano-Reggiano.

Per each of 6 servings 110 calories, 11 g protein, 6 g fat, 2 g carbohydrates, 0 g fiber

Noodle Soup

Zuppa di Pasta

2 cans (each 10 oz/284 mL) condensed chicken broth, undiluted	1 red bell pepper, diced
	1/3 cup (75 mL) chopped fresh Italian parsley
4 cups (1 L) water	1/4 cup (50 mL) freshly grated
4 oz (125 g) spaghetti, broken	Parmigiano-Reggiano cheese

In a large saucepan, bring chicken broth and water to a boil over high heat. Add spaghetti and boil gently for about 5 minutes or until al dente (tender but firm to the bite). Stir in red pepper, parsley and cheese. Reduce heat and simmer for 5 minutes to allow flavors to blend.

VARIATIONS

Egg and Noodle Soup: Omit red pepper. In a bowl, using a fork, beat 4 eggs with the cheese and parsley. Slowly pour into simmering stock, stirring constantly, and simmer, stirring, for 2 minutes or until eggs are set.

Chicken and Noodle Soup: Dice 2 boneless skinless chicken breasts and add to soup with red pepper, cheese and parsley. Simmer for about 8 minutes or until chicken is no longer pink inside.

Per serving 200 calories, 14 g protein, 4 g fat, 26 g carbohydrates, 2 g fiber

Passatelli Soup

Passatelli in Brodo

3 eggs, lightly beaten
1 cup (250 mL) freshly grated
  Parmigiano-Reggiano cheese
Pinch salt
Pinch freshly ground black pepper

1 cup (250 mL) dry Italian-seasoned
  bread crumbs
6 cups (1.5 L) vegetable or chicken
  stock (store-bought or see recipe,
  page 22)

Makes 4 servings

Homemade pasta can take some time to prepare, but not these quick little noodles. By mixing together eggs, cheese and bread, you create a savory noodle that needs only a simple stock to enjoy with it. You can make the noodles in the morning and refrigerate them to cook for dinner that night, but it's easy enough to make them right before dinner.

In a large bowl, using a fork, stir together eggs, cheese, salt and pepper. Add bread crumbs and mix together with hands to form smooth dough. Using the palms of your hands, roll ½ tsp (2 mL) of the dough into a thin strand. Set on a plate. Repeat with remaining dough.

Meanwhile, in a large saucepan, bring stock to a simmer. Add noodles and cook, stirring gently, for about 5 minutes or until noodles are firm and float to the top.

Per serving 330 calories, 27 g protein, 14 g fat, 24 g carbohydrates, 1 g fiber

Cooked Water Soup

Acqua Cotta

Makes 6 servings

I enjoyed this soup in Maremma, in a small family-owned restaurant. Local farmers ask for this family soup on cool nights, but it also works as a quick lunchtime treat.

Tips

To poach eggs, fill a shallow saucepan or deep skillet halfway with water. Bring to a boil and add 1 tbsp (15 mL) white vinegar. Reduce heat to a simmer. Crack eggs one at a time, gently slip into water and cook for about 3 minutes or until desired doneness. With a slotted spoon, remove eggs to a plate lined with paper towels. Cover with plastic wrap to keep warm or gently slip into cold water to chill and refrigerate for up to 24 hours. Reheat in simmering water or in the microwave.

Top each poached egg with salt, pepper and freshly grated Parmigiano-Reggiano.

2 tbsp (25 mL) extra-virgin olive oil	4 cups (1 L) chicken or vegetable stock (store-bought or see recipe, page 22)
2 stalks celery, finely chopped	
1 onion, finely chopped	2 eggs
1 carrot, finely chopped	2 tbsp (25 mL) freshly grated Parmigiano-Reggiano cheese
½ tsp (2 mL) hot pepper flakes	
2 pkgs (10 oz/300 g each) fresh baby spinach	6 slices crusty Italian bread, toasted or grilled
1 can (19 oz/540 mL) diced tomatoes	6 eggs, poached (see tip, at left) (optional)

In a large Dutch oven, heat oil over medium heat. Add celery, onion, carrot and hot pepper flakes; cook, stirring, for about 5 minutes or until vegetables are softened. Add spinach and cook, stirring, for about 3 minutes or until spinach is wilted and bright green. Add tomatoes and stock; bring to a boil. Reduce heat, cover and simmer for 20 minutes to allow flavors to blend.

Meanwhile, in a small bowl, whisk together eggs and cheese. Add to soup and simmer, stirring constantly, for about 3 minutes or until slightly thickened. (*Can be refrigerated for up to 1 day. Reheat before continuing.*)

Place 1 slice of bread in each of 6 bowls. Ladle soup over bread and top with poached egg, if using.

Per serving 220 calories, 12 g protein, 9 g fat, 22 g carbohydrates, 4 g fiber

Minestrone Soup

Minestrone

1 tbsp (15 mL) extra-virgin olive oil
4 oz (125 g) pancetta, chopped
4 cloves garlic, minced
2 carrots, chopped
1 onion, chopped
1 stalk celery, chopped
1 tbsp (15 mL) dried oregano
½ tsp (2 mL) hot pepper flakes
¼ tsp (1 mL) salt
¼ tsp (1 mL) freshly ground black
  pepper

1 can (28 oz/796 mL) diced tomatoes
6 cups (1.5 L) chicken stock (store-
  bought or see recipe, page 22)
1 pkg (10 oz/300 g) fresh baby
  spinach
1 can (19 oz/540 mL) romano beans,
  drained and rinsed
1 cup (250 mL) ditali or tubetti pasta
⅓ cup (75 mL) chopped fresh Italian
  parsley
2 tbsp (25 mL) chopped fresh basil

Makes 6 servings

This soup is a classic in every Italian home, and each family has its own recipe. The hot pepper flakes add a hint of spice.

In a large saucepan, heat oil over medium-high heat. Add pancetta and cook for 2 minutes or until crisp. Reduce heat to medium. Add garlic, carrots, onion, celery, oregano, hot pepper flakes, salt and pepper; cook for about 5 minutes or until vegetables are softened.

Add tomatoes and stock; bring to a boil. Add spinach, beans and pasta; reduce heat, cover and simmer for about 20 minutes or until pasta is tender. Stir in parsley and basil. (*Can be refrigerated for up to 2 days. Reheat before serving.*)

Per serving 390 calories, 22 g protein, 11 g fat, 51 g carbohydrates, 13 g fiber

Vegetable Soup with Pesto

Zuppa Vegetale con Pesto

Makes 6 servings

Lesleigh Landry, one of my great friends, was one of the first free-lance food people I met when I came to Toronto, and we clicked right away—I think we must be related! She is definitely an honorary Italian. Lesleigh shares her love of cooking with everyone she meets. She offers up this quick and easy soup that any family will enjoy on a busy weeknight.

Tips

Chicken stock gives a rounded flavor to this soup, but if you are serving vegetarians use vegetable stock.

If you can't find low-sodium stock, add more water to dilute canned stock, or use homemade stock.

1 tbsp (15 mL) extra-virgin olive oil
3 carrots, sliced
2 onions, chopped
2 stalks celery, sliced
7 cups (1.75 L) low-sodium chicken or vegetable stock (store-bought or see recipe, page 22)
¾ cup (175 mL) pastina (such as mini shells, orzo or ditali)
¼ cup (50 mL) pesto (store-bought or see recipe, page 18)

In a large saucepan, heat oil over medium heat. Add carrots, onions and celery; cook, stirring occasionally, for about 5 minutes or until softened. Increase heat to medium-high, add stock and bring to a boil. Stir in pastina and cook, stirring occasionally, for 5 to 10 minutes or until pastina is tender but firm. (*Can be refrigerated for up to 3 days. Reheat before adding pesto.*)

Ladle into bowls and top with a dollop of pesto.

VARIATION
Add 2 cups (500 mL) chopped smoked sausage or ham with pastina.

Per serving 220 calories, 9 g protein, 9 g fat, 25 g carbohydrates, 3 g fiber

Ricotta Ball Soup

Zuppa di Polpette di Ricotta

12 cups (3 L) chicken or vegetable stock (store-bought or see recipe, page 22)
⅓ cup (75 mL) chopped fresh Italian parsley
1 tub (16 oz/454 g) ricotta cheese
1 egg

1 cup (250 mL) dry bread crumbs (approx)
⅓ cup (75 mL) shredded mozzarella cheese
¼ cup (50 mL) freshly grated Parmigiano-Reggiano cheese
¼ tsp (1 mL) salt

Makes 4 to 6 servings

This soup is traditionally made at Easter, but is delicious year-round. The ricotta balls are moist and delicate, and make spooning the soup into your mouth that much more enjoyable. *Mangia!*

In a large stockpot or Dutch oven, bring stock and 3 tbsp (45 mL) of the parsley to a boil. Reduce heat to a simmer.

Meanwhile, in a large bowl, stir together ricotta cheese, egg, half of the bread crumbs, mozzarella cheese, Parmigiano-Reggiano cheese, the remaining parsley and salt. Add enough of the remaining bread crumbs to help mixture stick together. Shape mixture into 2-inch (5 cm) balls.

Using a slotted spoon or ladle, gently add ricotta balls to stock. Return stock to a simmer and cook for about 10 minutes or until ricotta balls are firm throughout.

Per each of 6 servings 330 calories, 26 g protein, 17 g fat, 19 g carbohydrates, 1 g fiber

Tortellini Soup

Zuppa di Tortellini

1 lb (500 g) fresh or frozen meat or cheese tortellini
8 cups (2 L) chicken or vegetable stock (store-bought or see recipe, page 22)

2 tbsp (25 mL) chopped fresh Italian parsley or basil
¼ cup (50 mL) freshly grated Parmigiano-Reggiano cheese

In a large pot of boiling salted water, cook tortellini for 8 minutes or until they float to the top. Drain and set aside.

Meanwhile, in a large saucepan, bring stock and parsley to a boil. Stir in tortellini, reduce heat and simmer for 5 minutes.

Ladle into deep soup bowls and sprinkle with cheese.

Per serving 460 calories, 27 g protein, 15 g fat, 53 g carbohydrates, 1 g fiber

Mini Meatball Soup

Zuppa di Polpettine

8 oz (250 g) lean ground veal
⅓ cup (75 mL) freshly grated
  Parmigiano-Reggiano cheese
3 tbsp (45 mL) chopped fresh Italian
  parsley
Pinch salt

Pinch freshly ground black pepper
6 cups (1.5 L) chicken stock (store-
  bought or see recipe, page 22)
¼ cup (50 mL) fresh Italian parsley
  leaves
½ cup (125 mL) pastina

In a bowl, using your hands, combine veal, cheese, chopped parsley, salt and pepper. Roll by mounded teaspoons (5 mL) into balls; place on a large plate.

Meanwhile, in a large saucepan, bring stock and parsley leaves to a boil. Add pastina and boil gently for 8 minutes. Using a slotted spoon or ladle, add meatballs; simmer for about 7 minutes or until pastina is tender and meatballs are no longer pink inside.

VARIATION
For some extra greens, add 2 cups (500 mL) finely shredded fresh spinach with the meatballs.

Makes 4 servings

This kids' favorite will appeal to grown-ups too. The little meatballs can be made ahead and frozen to add to this soup or to pasta sauce for another night.

Tips

If you want to add the meatballs to a pasta sauce, boil them gently in the sauce for about 15 minutes or until no longer pink inside.

If your ground veal was previously frozen, and you want to freeze the meatballs, be sure to bake them first in a 350°F (180°C) oven for about 8 minutes or until no longer pink inside. (Or cook in a nonstick skillet over medium-high heat, shaking pan gently, for about 10 minutes.) Let cool completely, place in an airtight container and freeze for up to 1 month.

Per serving   260 calories, 25 g protein, 9 g fat, 19 g carbohydrates, 1 g fiber

Mussel Soup

Zuppa di Cozze

Makes 4 servings

Nothing brings you the flavors of the Mediterranean like mussel soup. Many coastal provinces throughout Italy celebrate their abundance of seafood in simple soups such as this one. You'll need crusty bread to sop up the remaining juices in the bowl.

Tip

Check mussels before adding them to the soup. The shells should be tightly closed. If a shell is slightly open, give it a little tap; if it doesn't close, discard it. Once they are cooked, discard any that have not opened. This gives you two chances to get rid of the bad ones.

2 tbsp (25 mL) extra-virgin olive oil
3 cloves garlic, minced
1 onion, finely chopped
½ cup (125 mL) chopped fresh Italian parsley
½ tsp (2 mL) hot pepper flakes
4 lbs (2 kg) mussels, rinsed
1 cup (250 mL) dry white wine

1 cup (250 mL) chicken stock (store-bought or see recipe, page 22) or fish stock
2 tbsp (25 mL) all-purpose flour
2 tbsp (25 mL) butter, softened
Pinch salt
8 baguette slices, toasted
1 lemon, cut in wedges

In a large stockpot or Dutch oven, heat oil over medium heat. Add garlic, onion, half of the parsley and hot pepper flakes; cook for about 5 minutes or until onion is softened. Add mussels, cover and cook for about 10 minutes or until mussels open. Add wine and stock; simmer for 10 minutes to allow flavors to blend.

With a slotted spoon, remove mussels and divide them among 4 large deep bowls.

In a small bowl, mix together flour and butter to make a paste. Whisk into soup and bring to a boil. Add salt.

Ladle soup over mussels and sprinkle with the remaining parsley. Garnish with baguette slices and lemon wedges.

VARIATION

This soup is also delicious with 2 lbs (1 kg) mussels and 2 lbs (1 kg) jumbo shrimp, peeled and deveined.

Per serving 420 calories, 28 g protein, 18 g fat, 28 g carbohydrates, 2 g fiber

Italian Express

Tuscan White Bean Soup

Zuppa di Fagioli Bianchi alla Toscana

1 tbsp (15 mL) extra-virgin olive oil
4 cloves garlic, minced
1 onion, chopped
1 carrot, chopped
1 stalk celery, chopped
1 tsp (5 mL) crumbled dried sage
2 cans (each 19 oz/540 mL) white
  kidney or romano beans, drained
  and rinsed

6 cups (1.5 L) vegetable or chicken
  stock (store-bought or see recipe,
  page 22)
4 cups (1 L) lightly packed shredded
  kale
Pinch salt
Pinch freshly ground black pepper

Makes 4 servings

I tried a similar soup in Tuscany and fell in love with its strong, earthy taste. This version is easy to prepare and has a rustic feel to it.

In a large saucepan, heat oil over medium heat. Add garlic, onion, carrot, celery and sage; cook for 5 minutes or until vegetables are softened. Add beans, stock, kale, salt and pepper; cover and cook, stirring occasionally, for about 20 minutes or until kale is tender. (*Cover and refrigerate for up to 1 day. Reheat before serving.*)

VARIATIONS
Try using other types of canned beans.

Substitute spinach or rapini for the kale.

Per serving 410 calories, 28 g protein, 7 g fat, 59 g carbohydrates, 15 g fiber

Beans and Pasta Soup

Pasta e Fagioli

Makes 4 to 6 servings

Beans and pasta in a rich, hearty broth make up this famous home-cooked peasant soup.

Tip

Feel free to use your favorite beans, such as red kidney beans, chickpeas or romano beans, in place of the white kidney beans.

4 oz (125 g) pancetta, diced
4 cloves garlic, minced
2 stalks celery, chopped
1 onion, chopped
¼ tsp (1 mL) hot pepper flakes
1 can (28 oz/796 mL) tomatoes
2 cups (500 mL) vegetable or chicken
  stock (store-bought or see recipe,
  page 22)
1 can (19 oz/540 mL) white kidney
  beans, drained and rinsed
1 cup (250 mL) ditali or tubetti pasta
2 tbsp (25 mL) chopped fresh basil

In a large saucepan, cook pancetta over medium-high heat for about 3 minutes or until golden. Add garlic, celery, onion and hot pepper flakes; cook for about 5 minutes or until vegetables are softened.

Meanwhile, in a blender or food processor, purée tomatoes until smooth. Pour into vegetable mixture, add stock and bring to a boil. Reduce heat, and simmer for 10 minutes. Add beans, ditali and basil; simmer for 8 to 10 minutes or until pasta is al dente (tender but firm to the bite).

Per each of 6 servings 310 calories, 17 g protein, 8 g fat, 44 g carbohydrates, 7 g fiber

Swiss Chard with Romano Bean Soup

Zuppa di Bietola e Fagioli

6 cups (1.5 L) water
8 cups (2 L) lightly packed shredded
  Swiss chard
1 tbsp (15 mL) extra-virgin olive oil
2 cloves garlic, minced
1 onion, chopped

Pinch hot pepper flakes
1 can (19 oz/540 mL) romano beans,
  drained and rinsed
2 cups (500 mL) chicken stock
  (store-bought or see recipe, page 22)

Makes 4 servings

Greens are bountiful during the fall and winter months, so why not enjoy them? Chopped up in soup and served with crusty bread, greens are a heart-warming supper.

In a large saucepan, bring water to a boil. Add Swiss chard and cook for 5 minutes or until bright green. Drain Swiss chard, reserving water.

In the same saucepan, heat oil over medium heat. Add garlic, onion and hot pepper flakes; cook for 2 minutes or until onion is softened. Add Swiss chard, 2 cups (500 mL) of the reserved water, beans and stock; bring to a boil. Reduce heat and simmer for 10 minutes or until Swiss chard is very tender.

VARIATION
Substitute spinach or escarole for the Swiss chard.

Per serving 210 calories, 13 g protein, 4.5 g fat, 30 g carbohydrates, 12 g fiber

Calabrian Cooked Bread Soup

Pane Cotto Calabrese

Makes 4 to 6 servings

This cooked bread soup has tons of flavor from the pancetta and tomatoes. With the optional sliced sausage, it's a filling meal on its own.

Tips

If the pancetta doesn't render very much fat in which to cook the onion, add 1 tbsp (15 mL) of extra-virgin olive oil to the pan before adding onion.

Use chicory, rapini, spinach or Swiss chard for the greens. Whichever you choose, make sure it's the freshest!

4 oz (125 g) pancetta, diced
2 cloves garlic, minced
1 small onion, finely chopped
1 stalk celery, finely chopped
¼ cup (50 mL) chopped fresh Italian parsley
1 can (28 oz/796 mL) diced tomatoes
4 cups (1 L) chicken stock (store-bought or see recipe, page 22)
4 cups (1 L) lightly packed thinly sliced greens
2 thick slices stale Italian bread, chopped
3 tbsp (45 mL) freshly grated pecorino Romano cheese
2 Italian sausages, cooked and sliced (optional)
Extra-virgin olive oil (optional)

In a large saucepan, cook pancetta over medium-high heat for about 3 minutes or until beginning to turn golden. Reduce heat to medium and add garlic, onion, celery and parsley; cook for about 5 minutes or until vegetables are softened.

Add tomatoes and stock; bring to a boil. Reduce heat, and simmer for 15 minutes. Add greens and bread; simmer, stirring, for about 8 minutes or until greens are tender and bread is soft. (*Can be refrigerated for up to 2 days. Reheat before continuing.*)

Ladle into soup bowls and sprinkle with cheese. Top with sliced sausages and drizzle with olive oil, if using.

Per each of 6 servings 190 calories, 12 g protein, 8 g fat, 16 g carbohydrates, 4 g fiber

Hearty Tuscan Soup

Ribollita

1 tbsp (15 mL) extra-virgin olive oil
4 cloves garlic, minced
1 onion, chopped
1 carrot, chopped
1 stalk celery, thinly sliced
1 tsp (5 mL) dried thyme
¼ tsp (1 mL) hot pepper flakes
1 Yukon gold potato, peeled and diced
1 can (28 oz/796 mL) diced tomatoes
4 cups (1 L) chicken stock (store-bought or see recipe, page 22)

1 can (19 oz/540 mL) white kidney beans, drained and rinsed
6 cups (1.5 L) lightly packed shredded Swiss chard
¼ tsp (1 mL) salt
¼ tsp (1 mL) freshly ground black pepper
6 slices toasted Italian bread
¼ cup (50 mL) grated Parmigiano-Reggiano cheese

Makes 6 servings

This soup really hits the spot on a cold winter night. Depending on where you eat it in Italy, the soup is either thickened with bread or simply poured over bread. Either way, the broth is absorbed into the bread for a thick and hearty bowlful.

In a large saucepan, heat oil over medium heat. Add garlic, onion, carrot, celery, thyme and hot pepper flakes; cook for about 5 minutes or until vegetables are softened. Stir in potato, tomatoes and stock; bring to a boil. Reduce heat and boil gently for 15 minutes.

Add beans, Swiss chard, salt and pepper; simmer, stirring occasionally, for about 10 minutes or until Swiss chard is tender. (*Cover and refrigerate for up to 1 day. Reheat before continuing.*)

Place 1 slice of bread in each of 6 soup bowls. Ladle soup over bread and sprinkle with cheese.

VARIATION
Substitute Savoy cabbage, rapini or spinach for the Swiss chard.

Per serving 280 calories, 15 g protein, 6 g fat, 42 g carbohydrates, 9 g fiber

salad

Cold or warm, salads always have a place at my dinner table. The easy-to-make salads in this chapter run the gamut from light and refreshing to hearty and filling. Rich in tomatoes, garlic, tuna and herbs, these Italian favorites will be a hit with your family.

When you're looking for a dish to bring to a potluck or get-together, look no further: a salad with an Italian twist is a surefire winner. Try the Arugula and Roasted Pepper Pasta Salad (page 46) or the Layered Caprese Salad with Prosciutto (page 44). And give your family a midday protein boost by packing Tuna and Tomato Salad (page 48) in their lunchboxes.

Layered Caprese Salad with Prosciutto

Insalata di Bocconcini e Pomodoro

8 slices Italian bread, about ½ inch (1 cm) thick
¼ cup (50 mL) extra-virgin olive oil
¼ cup (50 mL) balsamic vinegar
4 tomatoes, thinly sliced
¼ tsp (1 mL) salt

8 bocconcini, sliced
16 thin slices prosciutto
¼ cup (50 mL) chopped pitted oil-cured black olives
¼ cup (50 mL) chopped fresh basil

Trim crusts from bread. Place half the bread in the bottom of an 8-inch (2 L) square casserole dish, trimming to fit as necessary.

Drizzle with 2 tbsp (25 mL) each of the oil and vinegar. Layer with half of the tomato slices, half of the salt, half of the bocconcini slices and half of the prosciutto slices. Repeat layers and drizzle with the remaining oil and vinegar. Sprinkle with olives and basil. Let stand for at least 15 minutes before serving. (*Cover and refrigerate for up to 1 day.*)

VARIATIONS

If you can find it, substitute Calabrese bread for the Italian bread.

For a slightly lighter and sweeter flavor, substitute white balsamic vinegar for the balsamic vinegar.

Per serving 400 calories, 18 g protein, 25 g fat, 26 g carbohydrates, 3 g fiber

Panzanella Salad

Insalata Panzanella

4 tomatoes

1 jar (12 oz/340 mL) roasted red bell
  peppers, drained

6 oz (175 g) sliced prosciutto,
  chopped

2 cups (500 mL) chopped toasted or
  grilled Italian bread (see tips, at
  right)

½ cup (125 mL) chopped fresh basil

1 small clove garlic, minced

¼ cup (50 mL) extra-virgin olive oil

3 tbsp (45 mL) red wine vinegar

1 tsp (5 mL) dried oregano

¼ tsp (1 mL) salt

¼ tsp (1 mL) freshly ground black
  pepper

Cut each tomato in half and remove most of the seeds. Chop into bite-size pieces and place in a large bowl. Slice red peppers into thin strips and add to bowl along with prosciutto, bread and basil.

In a small bowl, whisk together garlic, oil, vinegar, oregano, salt and pepper. Pour over salad and toss to coat. Let stand for 15 minutes before serving to allow bread to soften.

Makes 2 to 3 servings

Bread salads often seem heavy, with so much stale bread. In this salad, I have lightened up on the bread and added tons of tomatoes, a little prosciutto and roasted red peppers. This is summer on a plate.

Tips

To toast bread, place slices on a baking sheet and toast in a 400°F (200°C) oven, turning once, for about 10 minutes or until golden. Let cool.

To grill bread, brush both sides of slices with oil and place on a grill heated to medium-high, turning once, for about 5 minutes or until golden and crisp. Let cool.

Per each of 3 servings 490 calories, 22 g protein, 33 g fat, 26 g carbohydrates, 4 g fiber

Arugula and Roasted Pepper Pasta Salad

Insalata di Pasta con Peperoni Arrostiti e Rucola

Makes 4 servings

Arugula is crisp and peppery, a perfect match for roasted red peppers. To turn this salad into a full meal, add some chopped cooked chicken, turkey or ham.

4 cups (1 L) fusilli or penne pasta
1 bunch arugula, trimmed
1 jar (12 oz/340 mL) roasted red bell peppers, drained
2 jars (each 6 oz/170 mL) marinated artichokes, drained
4 green onions, chopped
2 tomatoes, seeded and chopped
1 clove garlic, minced
¼ cup (50 mL) white wine vinegar
3 tbsp (45 mL) extra-virgin olive oil
1 tbsp (15 mL) chopped fresh thyme
2 tsp (10 mL) Dijon mustard
¼ tsp (1 mL) salt
¼ tsp (1 mL) freshly ground black pepper
2 tbsp (25 mL) chopped fresh Italian parsley

In a large pot of boiling salted water, cook pasta for about 8 minutes or until al dente (tender but firm to the bite). Drain and rinse under cold water until pasta is cool; place in a large bowl.

Tear arugula into bite-size pieces and add to pasta. Slice red peppers into thin strips and add to pasta along with artichokes, green onions and tomatoes.

In a small bowl, whisk together garlic, vinegar, oil, thyme, mustard, salt and pepper. Pour over salad, add parsley and toss to coat. (*Cover and refrigerate for up to 1 day.*)

VARIATION
Substitute 6 cups (1.5 L) lightly packed fresh baby spinach or mesclun greens for the arugula.

Per serving 580 calories, 16 g protein, 20 g fat, 84 g carbohydrates, 11 g fiber

Marisa's Rice Salad

Insalata di Riso di Marisa

3 cups (750 mL) water
1½ cups (375 mL) long-grain
 converted (parboiled) rice
½ tsp (2 mL) salt
1 jar (12 oz/375 mL) giardiniera
 vegetables, drained (see tip, at right)

1 can (10 oz/284 mL) mushrooms,
 drained and rinsed
1 can (7 oz/199 mL) corn kernels,
 drained
½ cup (125 mL) diced pickles
½ cup (125 mL) light mayonnaise

Makes 4 to 6 servings

I never really enjoyed rice salad until I had it one evening at my cousin Marisa's house. I couldn't help but have three—okay, four—servings. Make this salad heartier by mixing in cooked chicken or tuna. For a little kick, add some freshly ground black pepper.

In a medium saucepan, bring water, rice and salt to a boil. Reduce heat to low, cover and simmer for about 20 minutes or until water is evaporated and rice is tender. Transfer to a large bowl.

Meanwhile, chop giardiniera vegetables into bite-size pieces. Add to rice along with mushrooms, corn and pickles; stir to combine. Add mayonnaise and toss to coat. (*Cover and refrigerate for up to 2 days.*)

VARIATIONS

Substitute a small can (14 oz/398 mL) of mini corncobs for the corn kernels.

Add 2 cups (500 mL) cooked shredded or chopped chicken.

Add 2 cans (each 4 oz/120 g) of tuna or salmon, drained.

Add 4 oz (125 g) chopped prosciutto and 2 plum tomatoes, chopped.

Tip

Giardiniera vegetables are a mixture of pickled garden vegetables—such as carrots, cauliflower, celery and bell peppers—and some olives and pearl onions. Look for them in the same section of the grocery store as the olives and pickles.

Per each of 6 servings 300 calories, 5 g protein, 7 g fat, 54 g carbohydrates, 3 g fiber

Tuna and Tomato Salad

Insalata di Tonno e Pomodoro

Makes 4 servings

This salad makes a nice light dinner on a summer night, but it also packs well for lunch. Serve it with some crusty Italian buns, or fill them with salad and add a few lettuce leaves for a great sandwich. Alternatively, use the salad as bruschetta topping on toasted crostini.

Tip

Always taste your olives for saltiness. If they are too salty, give them a quick rinse before using them.

4 vine-ripened tomatoes, chopped
1 yellow bell pepper, chopped
1 stalk celery, thinly sliced
⅓ cup (75 mL) halved pitted
  oil-cured black olives
1 tbsp (15 mL) capers
2 cans (each 3 oz/80 g) tuna in olive
  oil, drained

¼ cup (50 mL) chopped fresh basil
1 small clove garlic, minced
3 tbsp (45 mL) extra-virgin olive oil
1 tbsp (15 mL) red wine vinegar
1 tsp (5 mL) dried oregano
Pinch salt
Pinch freshly ground black pepper

In a large bowl, toss together tomatoes, yellow pepper, celery, olives and capers. Sprinkle with tuna and basil.

In a small bowl, whisk together garlic, oil, vinegar, oregano, salt and pepper. Pour over salad and toss to coat. (*Cover and refrigerate for up to 4 hours.*)

Per serving 240 calories, 12 g protein, 17 g fat, 10 g carbohydrates, 3 g fiber

Paola's Tuna and Potato Salad

Insalata di Tonno e Patate di Paola

4 Yukon gold potatoes, peeled (about 1 lb/500 g total)

2 cans (each 3 oz/80 g) tuna in olive oil, drained

1 green bell pepper, chopped

⅓ cup (75 mL) thinly sliced red onion

¼ cup (50 mL) light mayonnaise

2 tbsp (25 mL) extra-virgin olive oil

2 tbsp (25 mL) finely chopped oil-packed sun-dried tomatoes

1 tbsp (15 mL) capers

1 anchovy fillet, finely minced

¼ tsp (1 mL) freshly ground black pepper

Pinch salt

1 tbsp (15 mL) chopped fresh Italian parsley

Makes 2 servings

Tuna is eaten frequently throughout Italy. Tuna packed in olive oil has the best flavor—it is so much more tender than tuna packed in water. Drain the oil (use it to flavor bread, if desired), so the tuna is not too rich. Try it in your next tuna sandwich, or in any of these salad recipes, and taste the Italian difference.

Tip

Tuna packed in olive oil comes in smaller tins than tuna packed in water, but you can find it in the same part of the grocery store.

Cut potatoes into 2-inch (5 cm) chunks. Add to a large pot of water and bring to a boil. Boil gently for about 15 minutes or until potatoes are tender but firm. Drain well and place in a large bowl. Add tuna, green pepper and red onion.

In a small bowl, whisk together mayonnaise, oil, tomatoes, capers, anchovy, pepper and salt. Scrape onto salad and toss to coat well. Sprinkle with parsley. (*Cover and refrigerate for up to 1 day.*)

VARIATION

Substitute 1 tsp (5 mL) anchovy paste for the anchovy fillet.

Per serving 650 calories, 28 g protein, 31 g fat, 65 g carbohydrates, 7 g fiber

Tuna and White Bean Salad

Insalata di Tonno e Fagioli Bianchi

Makes 2 to 3 servings

I saw this salad in a number of places in Naples, where it was served with a wedge of lemon. Spritz the salad with lemon juice just before eating for an added zip of freshness.

2 cans (each 3 oz/80 g) tuna in olive oil, drained
1 can (19 oz/540 mL) white kidney beans, drained and rinsed
1 red bell pepper, thinly sliced
6 cups (1.5 L) lightly packed fresh baby spinach or arugula

3 tbsp (45 mL) extra-virgin olive oil
2 tbsp (25 mL) freshly squeezed lemon juice
¼ tsp (1 mL) salt
¼ tsp (1 mL) freshly ground black pepper
2 to 3 lemon wedges

In a large bowl, toss together tuna, beans, red pepper and spinach.

In a small bowl, whisk together oil, lemon juice, salt and pepper. Pour over salad and toss to coat.

Divide among plates and garnish each with a lemon wedge.

Per each of 3 servings 430 calories, 28 g protein, 19 g fat, 37 g carbohydrates, 12 g fiber

Italian Green Bean Salad

Insalata di Fagioli Verde

1 lb (500 g) flat green beans, trimmed
3 plum tomatoes, chopped
2 cloves garlic, slivered
2 tbsp (25 mL) extra-virgin olive oil
2 tbsp (25 mL) balsamic vinegar
1 tbsp (15 mL) pesto (store-bought or
  see recipe, page 18)
1 tsp (5 mL) Dijon mustard

¼ tsp (1 mL) salt
1 tbsp (15 mL) chopped fresh Italian
  parsley
1 tbsp (15 mL) chopped fresh mint

Makes 4 servings

This dish is best in the summer, when flat green beans (also known as Italian green beans) are in season. At other times of the year, regular green beans work fine.

Tip

If using regular green beans, simply cut in half crosswise if they are more than 4 inches (8 cm) long.

Cut beans in half crosswise, then cut each half lengthwise to make thin strips. In a large pot of boiling salted water, cook beans for 8 minutes or until tender. Drain and rinse under cold water. Place in a large bowl and add tomatoes and garlic.

In a small bowl, whisk together oil, vinegar, pesto, mustard and salt. Pour over bean mixture and toss to coat. Sprinkle with parsley and mint; toss gently.

VARIATION
For a protein boost, add 2 chopped grilled chicken or salmon fillets.

Per serving 150 calories, 3 g protein, 9 g fat, 13 g carbohydrates, 4 g fiber

Warm Mushroom and Shrimp Salad

Insalata Calda di Funghi e Gamberi

¼ cup (50 mL) extra-virgin olive oil
1 clove garlic, minced
8 oz (250 g) cremini mushrooms, thinly sliced
¼ tsp (1 mL) salt
¼ tsp (1 mL) freshly ground black pepper
8 oz (250 g) cooked small shrimp

2 tbsp (25 mL) chopped fresh Italian parsley
3 cups (750 mL) chopped romaine lettuce
2 tbsp (25 mL) freshly squeezed lemon juice
2 tbsp (25 mL) shredded Asiago cheese

In a nonstick skillet, heat 1 tbsp (15 mL) of the oil over medium-high heat. Add garlic, mushrooms and a pinch of salt and pepper; sauté for 5 minutes or until golden brown. Remove from heat and stir in shrimp and parsley. (*Cover and refrigerate for up to 8 hours if you want to serve it cold.*)

Arrange romaine on 2 dinner plates and top with shrimp mixture.

In a small bowl, whisk together the remaining oil, lemon juice and a pinch of salt and pepper. Drizzle over salads and sprinkle with cheese.

VARIATIONS
You can use white button mushrooms if cremini mushrooms are unavailable. This salad is also delicious with oyster mushrooms.

Substitute an equal amount of lightly packed fresh baby spinach for the romaine.

Per serving 440 calories, 32 g protein, 31 g fat, 8 g carbohydrates, 4 g fiber

Balsamic Vegetable Salad

Insalata di Vegetale Balsamico

2 red bell peppers, quartered
2 zucchini, sliced lengthwise
¼ cup (50 mL) extra-virgin olive oil
2 carrots, sliced lengthwise
1 eggplant
¼ cup (50 mL) chopped fresh mint
1 tbsp (15 mL) each chopped fresh
  basil and Italian parsley

Balsamic Dressing
⅓ cup (75 mL) white balsamic vinegar
¼ cup (50 mL) extra-virgin olive oil
1 tbsp (15 mL) pesto (store-bought or
  see recipe, page 18)
1 tbsp (15 mL) Dijon mustard
¾ tsp (4 mL) salt
¼ tsp (1 mL) pepper

Makes 6 to 8 servings

Sometimes I want nothing but vegetables and I love them grilled on the barbecue. Here is a salad I make often throughout the summer and fall when these vegetables are in season. It lasts well for a couple of days in the fridge and any leftovers are perfect tossed into some warm pasta for another meal or to serve as a side dish.

Tip

White balsamic vinegar is clear and a touch sweeter than regular balsamic vinegar. You may substitute regular balsamic vinegar if desired.

In large bowl combine peppers, zucchini and carrots and toss with half of the oil. Cut eggplant into ½-inch (1 cm) rounds and place in another bowl and drizzle with remaining oil. Place vegetables on greased grill over medium high heat and grill for about 15 minutes, turning occasionally or until golden brown. Return to bowl and let cool slightly. Chop coarsely and return to bowl.

Balsamic Dressing: In bowl, whisk together vinegar, oil, pesto, mustard, salt and pepper. Drizzle over vegetables. Add mint, basil and parsley and toss well to coat.

Per serving 270 calories, 3 g protein, 21 g fat, 16 g carbohydrates, 4 g fiber

bread and pizza

When it comes to making my family happy at dinner-time, pizza comes up a lot. Food is so much more fun when you can eat with your hands! You don't need to order out for a terrific pizza—at least, not all the time. Make pizza dough ahead and freeze it. Once you have your dough rolled, everybody can make their own pizzas with their favorite toppings. When I was small, Nana let me sprinkle on my own cheese, sausage and pepperoni. Now I enjoy doing the same with my son, who adores pizza, but just mushrooms and cheese, please.

All of the yummy dishes in this chapter are easy to make, and even easier to eat. Stuffed Bread (page 64), filled with meat and vegetables, is a surefire hit with meat eaters and a perfect tote-along for lunch. But one of the biggest hits with my family and friends is the deep-fried Calzones (page 62).

Poalona Pizza

Pizza Poalona

Makes one 14-inch
(35 cm) pizza
or 4 servings

I enjoyed pizza in
Aiello, Italy, my mom's
hometown, and to my
surprise all the pizzas
were served by the
meter. We ate about
3 meters between the
7 of us and had room
for dessert!

Tip

If you have a pizza stone, heat
it up with your oven and slide
the pizza onto it for a "wood-
burning oven" taste.

1 small eggplant, thinly sliced
¼ cup (50 mL) extra-virgin olive oil
1 lb (500 g) pizza dough (store-bought
  or see recipe, page 16)

4 slices prosciutto
½ cup (125 mL) ricotta cheese

Brush eggplant slices with about 3 tbsp (45 mL) of the oil. Grill over medium-high heat or roast in a 425°F (220°C) oven for about 20 minutes, turning once, or until golden and tender; set aside.

Punch dough down and knead gently. Stretch dough to fit a 14-inch (35 cm) round pizza pan. Brush with the remaining oil and top with eggplant and prosciutto slices. Dollop with cheese.

Bake in the center of a 425°F (220°C) oven for about 20 minutes or until golden brown.

Per each of 4 servings 520 calories, 14 g protein, 29 g fat, 50 g carbohydrates, 4 g fiber

Calabrian Cooked Bread Soup (p. 40)

Layered Caprese Salad with Prosciutto (p. 44)

Warm Mushroom and Shrimp Salad (p. 52)

Poalona Pizza (p. 56)

Stuffed Bread (p. 64)

Smoked Salmon Pasta (p. 72)

Rapini Pasta with Garlic Bread Crumbs (p. 88)

Zia Lina's Frittata (p. 107)

Roman Pizza

Pizza Roma

½ small eggplant (about 4 oz/ 125 g), thinly sliced lengthwise

1 zucchini (about 4 oz/125 g), thinly sliced lengthwise

3 tbsp (45 mL) extra-virgin olive oil

1 lb (500 g) pizza dough (store-bought or see recipe, page 16)

½ cup (125 mL) pasta sauce (store-bought or see recipe, page 20)

½ cup (125 mL) thinly sliced roasted red peppers

1 cup (250 mL) shredded provolone cheese

Makes one 14-inch (35 cm) pizza or 4 servings.

Sitting on a terrace, sipping a glass of Italian red wine, my husband, James, and I enjoyed this pizza while watching Romans and tourists walk the cobbled streets of Rome.

Brush eggplant and zucchini with oil. Grill over medium-high heat or roast, turning once, in a 425°F (220°C) oven for about 20 minutes for the eggplant and about 12 minutes for the zucchini or until golden and tender; set aside.

Punch dough down and knead gently. Stretch dough to fit a 14-inch (35 cm) round pizza pan. Spread dough with pasta sauce and top with eggplant, zucchini, peppers and sprinkle with cheese.

Bake in the center of a 425°F (220°C) oven for about 20 minutes or until golden brown.

Per each of 4 servings 480 calories, 15 g protein, 24 g fat, 51 g carbohydrates, 4 g fiber

Rustic Pizza

Pizza Rustica

Makes one 14-inch
(35 cm) pizza or
4 servings

On this rustic Italian
pizza classic deli
fare makes a perfect
topping.

Tips

Some store-bought pizza
doughs are more than 1½
lbs (750 g) so you can actually
make two pizzas from one
dough if desired.

Look for the cooked mari-
nated mushrooms in the deli
section to use on the pizza.
There are regular and spicy
versions. Drain any excess oil
before using.

Prosciutto cotto is available
in the deli and is a cooked
version of the classic prosciutto.

1 lb (500 g) pizza dough (store-bought or see recipe, page 16)
½ cup (125 mL) pasta sauce (store-bought or see recipe, page 20)
1 jar (6 oz/170 mL) marinated artichokes, drained and coarsely chopped
4 oz (125 g) prosciutto cotto, diced
1 cup (250 mL) cooked mushrooms
¼ cup (50 mL) pitted black olives
1 cup (250 mL) shredded mozzarella cheese

Punch dough down and knead gently. Stretch dough to fit a 14-inch (35 cm) round pizza pan. Spread with pasta sauce and top with artichokes, prosciutto, mushrooms and olives. Sprinkle evenly with cheese.

Bake in the center of a 425°F (220°C) oven for about 20 minutes or until golden brown.

Per each of 4 servings 480 calories, 20 g protein, 21 g fat, 52 g carbohydrates, 6 g fiber

Four Cheese Pizza

Pizza Quattro Formaggi

1 lb (500 g) pizza dough (store-
  bought or see recipe, page 16)
1 tbsp (15 mL) extra-virgin olive oil
½ cup (125 mL) shredded mozzarella
  cheese

½ cup (125 mL) crumbled
  Gorgonzola cheese
½ cup (125 mL) shredded Asiago
  cheese
¼ cup (50 mL) freshly grated
  Parmigiano-Reggiano cheese

**Makes one 14-inch
(35 cm) pizza or
4 servings**

No home should be
without a pizza recipe
that has only cheese as
a topping. This pizza
showcases some pow-
erhouse flavors like
Gorgonzola and
Asiago, but feel free to
use any of your own
favorites.

Punch dough down and knead gently. Stretch dough to fit a 14-inch (35 cm) round pizza pan. Brush with oil and sprinkle evenly with mozzarella, Gorgonzola, Asiago and Parmigiano-Reggiano cheeses.

Bake in the center of a 425°F (220°C) oven for about 20 minutes or until golden brown.

PIZZA STONES

Pizza stones are available in gourmet food shops and come in different shapes such as circles and squares. Most are made of terra cotta stone and need to be heated up in the oven. When you turn your oven on, make sure the pizza stone is already inside. You can place the stone in the center or the bottom third of the oven to bake the pizza.

Use a pizza peel (a wooden board with a handle) sprinkled with cornmeal or flour to slide the pizza onto the stone. Cook the pizza right on the stone, then use the pizza peel to remove the pizza.

Tip
If you don't have a pizza
stone, a vented pizza pan or a
pan with holes in it will help
give you a crisp pizza crust.

Per each of 4 servings 480 calories, 18 g protein, 26 g fat, 44 g carbohydrates, 2 g fiber

Puglian Pizza

Pizza Pugliese

1 lb (500 g) pizza dough (store-bought or see recipe, page 16)
2 tbsp (25 mL) extra-virgin olive oil (approx.)
2 small onions, very thinly sliced

1 cup (250 mL) shredded Romano cheese (see tip, at left)
1 tsp (5 mL) dried oregano
¼ tsp (1 mL) hot pepper flakes (optional)
Pinch freshly ground black pepper

Punch dough down and knead gently. Stretch dough to fit a 14-inch (35 cm) round pizza pan. Brush with oil and sprinkle evenly with onions, cheese, oregano and hot pepper flakes, if using. Drizzle with more olive oil, if desired.

Bake in the center of a 425°F (220°C) oven for about 25 minutes or until golden brown. Sprinkle with black pepper.

Per serving 460 calories, 15 g protein, 24 g fat, 47 g carbohydrates, 3 g fiber

Egg and Ricotta Pizza Squares

Pizzette di Ricotta ed Uova

1 lb (500 g) pizza or bread dough
  (store-bought or see recipe, page
  16)
2 tbsp (25 mL) extra-virgin olive oil
5 eggs
2 tubs (each 16 oz/454 g) ricotta
  cheese

½ cup (125 mL) freshly grated
  Parmigiano-Reggiano cheese
½ cup (125 mL) chopped fresh Italian
  parsley
½ tsp (2 mL) salt
½ tsp (2 mL) freshly ground black
  pepper

Makes 8 servings

This is a traditional Italian Easter dish, but I make it all year round. I like to serve it for brunch. Try cutting it into finger-size pieces and serving it as an appetizer.

On a lightly floured work surface, roll out dough to a 12- x 18-inch (24 x 36 cm) rectangle. Fit into a greased 11- x 17-inch (22 x 34 cm) baking sheet, with dough hanging slightly over the sides. Brush with oil and set aside.

In a large bowl, whisk together eggs, ricotta and Parmigiano-Reggiano cheeses, parsley, salt and pepper. Spread evenly on dough, smoothing top. Bring dough overhang in to secure egg mixture.

Bake in the bottom third of a 400°F (200°C) oven for about 25 minutes or until crust is golden and filling is firm and set.

VARIATION
Try adding 4 oz (125 g) finely chopped prosciutto, prosciutto cotto or mortadella to the filling. Or try 2 sausages, cooked and chopped, or 2 dry sausages packed in oil, chopped.

Per serving 460 calories, 25 g protein, 28 g fat, 28 g carbohydrates, 1 g fiber

Calzones

Calzoni

Makes 4 servings

In my experience, when you make pizza the family is happy, but when you make calzones (also known as panzerotti) the family is ecstatic! You can bake these stuffed pizzas in a 400°F (200°C) oven for about 20 minutes or until golden brown, but I prefer to fry them. Change the fillings to suit your taste.

Tips

To keep calzones warm for up to 20 minutes, place in a 300°F (150°C) oven.

To reheat calzones, unwrap and place on a baking sheet in a 400°F (200°C) oven for about 10 minutes.

1 lb (500 g) pizza dough (store-bought or see recipe, page 16)
1 small clove garlic, minced
¾ cup (175 mL) thick pasta or pizza sauce
½ tsp (2 mL) dried oregano
½ green bell pepper, thinly sliced
½ small onion, thinly sliced (optional)
1 cup (250 mL) sliced pepperoni
1 cup (250 mL) sliced mushrooms
2 cups (500 mL) shredded mozzarella or provolone cheese
Vegetable oil

Divide dough into 4 equal parts and roll each into a 9-inch (23 cm) circle. Cover each lightly a with clean tea towel.

In a small bowl, stir together garlic, pasta sauce and oregano. Spread sauce over half of each dough circle, leaving a ½-inch (1 cm) border. Top with green pepper, onion (if using), pepperoni and mushrooms. Sprinkle evenly with cheese. Brush edges of dough with a little water and fold dough over filling to form half-moons. Fold over edges slightly and pinch to seal.

In a deep-fryer or a large heavy saucepan, heat vegetable oil over medium heat to 375°F (190°C). Add 1 calzone at a time and cook, turning once, for about 5 minutes or until golden brown. Using tongs, remove to a plate lined with paper towels. Repeat with remaining calzones. (*Wrap and refrigerate for up to 2 days.*)

Per serving 740 calories, 23 g protein, 49 g fat, 51 g carbohydrates, 4 g fiber

DEEP-FRYING

Deep-frying, when done properly, can produce crisp, light food that is not laden with fat. If oil is kept at the right temperature (which varies depending on the recipe), the food doesn't absorb much fat. If your deep-fryer doesn't have a temperature gauge, use a deep-fat (candy) thermometer to make sure the oil stays at the right temperature as you cook. Instead of extra-virgin olive oil, use vegetable oil, which has a higher smoke point, will not break down as quickly and, when food is cooked at the right temperature, will not be absorbed into the food. Be sure to drain food when you remove it from the oil, then place it on paper towels, which will absorb any excess oil.

Stuffed Bread

Pane Ripieni

Makes 6 to 8 servings

I knew this recipe was a huge hit when my husband offered to take about half of it to work! By combining traditional pizza toppings a little differently, you make a splendid filling packed with meat and vegetables for this unique stuffed bread. Serve with salad for a perfect dinner. It makes a delicious hot sandwich when reheated the next day.

2 tbsp (25 mL) extra-virgin olive oil
1 onion, chopped
12 oz (375 g) lean ground veal or pork
1 tbsp (15 mL) dried oregano
Pinch hot pepper flakes
2 cups (500 mL) chopped broccoli
  (about 8 oz/250 g)
4 cups (1 L) lightly packed fresh baby
  spinach
Pinch salt

Pinch freshly ground black pepper
1 jar (12 oz/340 mL) roasted red bell
  peppers, drained and chopped or
  see box, page 65
⅓ cup (75 mL) chopped pitted oil-
  cured black olives
2 cups (500 mL) diced provolone
  cheese
1½ lbs (750 g) pizza or bread dough
  (store-bought or see recipe, page 16)

In large deep skillet, heat oil over medium-high heat. Add onion, veal, oregano and hot pepper flakes; cook for 5 minutes or until onion is softened and veal is cooked through. Add broccoli, cover and cook for 3 minutes or until bright green and tender-crisp. Add spinach, salt and black pepper; cook, stirring, for about 2 minutes or until spinach is wilted. Remove from heat and add red peppers and olives; stir to combine. Let cool slightly, then stir in cheese.

Meanwhile, on a lightly floured work surface, roll out dough to a 12- x 16-inch (30 x 40 cm) rectangle. Place on a large baking sheet lined with parchment paper and reshape. Mound meat mixture in center of dough, leaving a 2-inch (5 cm) border at the short ends and a 3-inch (8 cm) border at the long ends. Cut diagonal strips about 1 inch (2.5 cm) wide and 3 inches long into the long ends. Crisscross strips over filling to get a braided look.

Bake in a 400°F (200°C) oven for about 20 minutes or until golden brown. Let cool slightly before serving.

VARIATION

For a different flavor combination, substitute sausage meat for the ground veal and chopped Swiss chard for the spinach.

For a bitter bite, try rapini, also known as broccoli rabe, for the broccoli.

Tip

You can serve this with pasta sauce on the side, but it's great on its own as well.

ROASTING PEPPERS

Roast your own peppers when you have time. Place peppers on barbecue on high heat or under broiler and roast, turning occasionally for about 15 minutes or until blackened and blistered. Let cool until easy enough to handle. Remove outside charred skin, stem and seeds. Peppers can be placed in freezer bags or airtight container and frozen for up to 6 months.

For 1 jar (12 oz/375 g) of roasted peppers you will need 3 of your own roasted peppers.

Don't stop at red peppers; roast all kinds for a variety of color and flavor.

Per each of 8 servings 470 calories, 24 g protein, 24 g fat, 39 g carbohydrates, 4 g fiber

short pasta

I love pasta, no matter what the shape or size! The recipes in this chapter are versatile enough to use with any short pasta you may have in your pantry. Be adventurous and explore your grocery store and Italian delis—there's a lot of variety out there. Whether it is classic penne rigate (ridged quills), farfalle (bowties) or little stuffed pillows and purses of pasta such as gnocchi and ravioli, these little morsels are tasty tossed with either chunky tomato sauce or cream sauce. The cream-based sauces are perfect when you're entertaining, but don't save them just for that; show your family how much you love them by serving short pasta with cream sauce on a weeknight.

Pasta with Quick Butter Sage Sauce

Pasta con Salsa Rapida di Burro e Salvia

Makes 4 servings

This easy dish is a quick weeknight pick-me-up.

I love this sauce with cheese ravioli and with gnocchi.

1 lb (500 g) pasta
½ cup (125 mL) butter
10 fresh sage leaves, finely chopped
Pinch salt

Pinch freshly ground black pepper
3 tbsp (45 mL) grated Parmigiano-
  Reggiano cheese

In a large pot of boiling salted water, cook pasta for 8 to 10 minutes or until al dente (tender but firm to the bite). Drain and return to the pot. In a skillet, melt butter over medium heat. Add sage, salt and pepper and cook for 2 minutes or until fragrant. Toss with cooked pasta. Sprinkle with cheese; toss again. Serve immediately.

Per serving 590 calories, 15 g protein, 26 g fat, 74 g carbohydrates, 3 g fiber

Sun-Dried Tomato and Pesto Pasta

Pasta con Pomodoro Secco e Pesto

1 tbsp (15 mL) extra-virgin olive oil
2 cloves garlic, minced
1 small onion, finely chopped
1½ cups (375 mL) canned diced
   tomatoes, with juices
1 tsp (5 mL) dried oregano
½ tsp (2 mL) dried basil
¼ tsp (1 mL) salt
¼ tsp (1 mL) freshly ground black
   pepper

½ cup (125 mL) pesto (store-bought
   or see recipe, page 18)
¼ cup (50 mL) finely chopped
   drained oil-packed sun-dried
   tomatoes
2 tbsp (25 mL) capers
2 tbsp (25 mL) chopped fresh Italian
   parsley
12 oz (375 g) penne rigate
2 tbsp (25 mL) freshly grated
   Parmigiano-Reggiano cheese

Makes 4 servings

This quick pasta dish
is reminiscent of the
Italian favorites, show-
casing tomatoes, pep-
pers and herbs in the
sauce. For a twist to
the flavor, look for
roasted red pepper or
sun-dried tomato
pesto.

In a large skillet, heat oil over medium heat. Add garlic and onion; cook, stir-ring, for 3 minutes or until softened. Add tomatoes with juices, oregano, basil, salt and pepper; bring to a boil. Reduce heat, and simmer for 5 min-utes. Stir in pesto, sun-dried tomatoes, capers and parsley, and simmer for about 5 minutes or until thickened.

Meanwhile, in a large pot of boiling salted water, cook penne for about 10 minutes or until al dente (tender but firm to the bite). Drain and return to the pot. Add sauce and toss to coat. Transfer to a warm serving bowl and sprinkle with cheese.

VARIATION
Try other short pasta, such as rotini or shells.

Tips

Look for canned diced toma-toes so you don't have to dice them yourself.

For 12 oz (375 g) penne, you will need 4 cups (1 L) dried pasta.

Per serving 590 calories, 20 g protein, 21 g fat, 80 g carbohydrates, 7 g fiber

Pasta with Zucchini Flowers

Pasta con Fiori di Zucchini

Makes 4 servings

If you grow zucchini, sometimes you just don't know what to do with all those flowers. They taste great fried in Pesce Fritto batter (see recipe, page 182) to make a crisp fritter, but they are also delicious in pasta. Here they are matched with their fruit for a light summer pasta dish.

Tips

If fresh zucchini flowers are not available, add 1 yellow zucchini, finely chopped, with the other zucchini.

For 12 oz (375 g) penne, you will need 4 cups (1 L) dried pasta.

12 oz (375 g) penne rigate
1/3 cup (75 mL) extra-virgin olive oil
2 cloves garlic, minced
1 zucchini, finely chopped (about 4 oz/125 g)
1/4 tsp (1 mL) salt
1/4 tsp (1 mL) hot pepper flakes
3 cups (750 mL) fresh zucchini flowers, chopped
1/4 cup (50 mL) chopped fresh Italian parsley

In a large pot of boiling salted water, cook penne for about 10 minutes or until al dente (tender but firm to the bite). Drain and return to the pot.

Meanwhile, in a large nonstick skillet, heat oil over medium-high heat. Add garlic, zucchini, salt and hot pepper flakes; cook, stirring, for about 5 minutes or until zucchini is softened and golden. Add zucchini flowers and parsley; cook, stirring, for about 2 minutes or until flowers are wilted. Pour over pasta and toss to coat.

VARIATION

Add 8 oz (250 g) large shrimp, peeled and deveined, to zucchini mixture and cook until pink and opaque.

Per serving 550 calories, 13 g protein, 21 g fat, 77 g carbohydrates, 4 g fiber

LOVE YOUR PASTA

Store your pasta in its original packaging when you get home, or you can transfer it to an airtight container. I prefer to transfer smaller pastas to clear glass jars so I can see how much I have and what shapes they are.

Buying large bags of dried pasta can sometimes be a bargain, but make sure you buy a kind you like to eat! If you have little bits of pasta left in your bags and boxes, you can make your own mix. Combine similar sizes and shapes so they will cook in the same amount of time. My son thinks it's pretty cool, because you can't buy that kind of pasta in the store—it's a simple idea that can impress.

Smoked Salmon Pasta

Pasta al Salmone Affumicato

Makes 4 servings

In Italy this is a favorite dish to serve guests because it's elegant, not too expensive and quick, all at the same time. Fresh fish can be very expensive, but a little bit of smoked salmon goes a long way and imparts tons of flavor. Use your favorite short pasta.

Tip

For 1 lb (500 g) farfalle, you will need 6 cups (1.5 L) dried pasta.

1 tbsp (15 mL) butter
1 clove garlic, minced
1/3 cup (75 mL) finely chopped red onion
6 oz (175 g) sliced smoked salmon
1 1/2 cups (375 mL) whipping (35%) cream
1/2 cup (125 mL) pasta sauce (store-bought or see recipe, page 20)
1 lb (500 g) farfalle
Pinch salt
Pinch freshly ground black pepper

In a large deep skillet, melt butter over medium heat. Add garlic and onion; cook, stirring, for about 2 minutes or until softened. Add smoked salmon, breaking it up with a spoon, and cook for 5 minutes. Add whipping cream and pasta sauce; bring to a boil. Reduce heat and boil gently, uncovered, for about 5 minutes or until sauce is thick enough to coat the back of spoon.

Meanwhile, in a large pot of boiling salted water, cook farfalle for about 8 minutes or until al dente (tender but firm to the bite). Drain and stir into sauce. Increase heat to medium and add salt and pepper; stir until well combined.

VARIATION
Substitute 1 shallot, finely chopped, for the red onion.

Per serving 780 calories, 23 g protein, 40 g fat, 81 g carbohydrates, 4 g fiber

Orecchiette with Fried Cauliflower and Pancetta

Orecchiette con Cavolofiore Fritto e Pancetta

1 lb (500 g) cauliflower, cut in bite-size pieces
⅓ cup (75 mL) extra-virgin olive oil
2 large cloves garlic, minced
4 oz (125 g) pancetta, chopped
12 oz (375 g) orecchiette
2 tbsp (25 mL) chopped fresh Italian parsley
¼ tsp (1 mL) salt
¼ tsp (1 mL) freshly ground black pepper
¼ cup (50 mL) freshly grated pecorino Romano cheese

In a large pot of boiling salted water, cook cauliflower for about 7 minutes or until just tender-crisp. Drain well and set aside.

In a large skillet, heat oil over medium heat. Add garlic and cook, stirring, for about 3 minutes or until softened. Add pancetta and cook, stirring, for 5 minutes or until browned. Add cauliflower and cook, stirring, for about 10 minutes or until starting to turn golden.

Meanwhile, in a large pot of boiling salted water, cook orecchiette for 8 to 10 minutes or until al dente (tender but firm to the bite). Drain and return to the pot. Add cauliflower sauce and toss to coat. Add parsley, salt and pepper and toss to combine. Transfer to a warm serving bowl and sprinkle with cheese.

Makes 4 servings

When it comes to pasta, Daphna Rabinovitch can cook with the best Italians. She loves to combine different flavors with her pasta. Daphna adores cauliflower and is always on the lookout for new ways to serve it. Here is one of her family's favorites.

Tips

For a chunkier sauce, buy a chunk of pancetta and dice it.

For 12 oz (375 g) orecchiette, you will need 4 cups (1 L) dried pasta.

Per serving 680 calories, 23 g protein, 31 g fat, 76 g carbohydrates, 6 g fiber

Farfalle Pasta with Pepper Cream Sauce

Farfalle con Salsa di Panna e Pepe

Makes 4 servings

This dish is perfect when peppers are in season. They have a sweet flavor that balances out the rich cream. To finish it off, you can sprinkle some cheese on top, but you will cover up the taste of the fresh basil and peppers.

Tip

For 1 lb (500 g) farfalle, you will need 6 cups (1.5 L) dried pasta.

2 tbsp (25 mL) butter
2 red bell peppers, diced
1 onion, finely chopped
1 cup (250 mL) whipping (35%)
  cream
¼ cup (50 mL) chopped fresh basil
¼ tsp (1 mL) salt
¼ tsp (1 mL) freshly ground black
  pepper
1 lb (500 g) farfalle

In a large nonstick skillet, melt butter over medium heat. Add red peppers and onion; cook, stirring, for about 10 minutes or until softened. Add whipping cream, basil, salt and pepper; bring to a boil. Reduce heat and simmer, uncovered, for 5 minutes or until slightly thickened.

Meanwhile, in a large pot of boiling salted water, cook farfalle for about 8 minutes or until al dente (tender but firm to the bite). Drain and return to the pot. Add sauce and toss to coat. Cook over low heat for 2 minutes.

Per serving 740 calories, 18 g protein, 30 g fat, 100 g carbohydrates, 6 g fiber

Mixed Vegetable Fusilli

Fusilli con Ortaggi Misti

1 small eggplant (about 8 oz/250 g)
2 small zucchini (about 12 oz/750 g total)
2 tbsp (25 mL) extra-virgin olive oil
1 cup (250 mL) vegetable stock (store-bought or see recipe, page 22)
4 plum tomatoes, chopped

2 cloves garlic, minced
¼ tsp (1 mL) salt
¼ tsp (1 mL) freshly ground black pepper
12 oz (375 g) fusilli
¼ cup (50 mL) freshly grated Parmigiano-Reggiano cheese

Makes 4 servings

This simple pasta dish was my *primo piatto* in Sorrento, a beautiful town where you can look across the bay and see the island of Capri. Small portions are perfect for a first course, but this has enough vegetables to satisfy your family for a full dinner.

Tip
For 12 oz (375 g) fusilli, you will need 4 cups (1 L) dried pasta.

Slice eggplant into thin slices; stack and cut into matchstick-size pieces. Cut zucchini into matchstick-size pieces.

In a large nonstick skillet, heat oil over medium-high heat. Add eggplant and cook, stirring, for about 6 minutes or until starting to turn golden. Add stock and bring to a boil. Add zucchini, tomatoes and garlic; cook, stirring, for about 10 minutes or until zucchini and eggplant are tender but firm and sauce is slightly thickened. Add salt and pepper.

Meanwhile, in a large pot of boiling salted water, cook fusilli for about 8 minutes or until al dente (tender but firm to the bite). Drain and return to the pot. Add sauce and cheese; toss to coat.

VARIATION
Try using carrots, broccoli, cherry tomatoes or other favorite vegetables to make your own vegetable creation.

Per serving 420 calories, 15 g protein, 11 g fat, 65 g carbohydrates, 6 g fiber

Vodka Penne

Penne alla Vodka

Makes 4 servings

This pasta has a splash of vodka, but not to worry—the alcohol cooks off. It's always a big hit with dinner guests, and it doesn't take long to make, which is great when everyone is hungry.

Tips

Purée tomatoes in a blender or food processor until smooth. For a chunkier version of the sauce, mash tomatoes with a potato masher instead.

For 1 lb (500 g) penne, you will need 6 cups (1.5 L) dried pasta.

1 tbsp (15 mL) butter	1 lb (500 g) penne rigate
1 small onion, finely chopped	2 tbsp (25 mL) chopped fresh basil
1 clove garlic, minced	½ tsp (2 mL) salt
¼ cup (50 mL) vodka	¼ tsp (1 mL) freshly ground black pepper
1 can (28 oz/796 mL) tomatoes, puréed (see tip, at left)	¼ cup (50 mL) freshly grated Parmigiano-Reggiano cheese
½ cup (125 mL) whipping (35%) cream	

In a large skillet, melt butter over medium heat. Add onion and garlic; cook, stirring, for about 5 minutes or until softened. Add vodka and bring to a boil. Add tomatoes and whipping cream; bring to a boil. Reduce heat and simmer, uncovered, for about 15 minutes or until slightly thickened.

Meanwhile, in a large pot of boiling salted water, cook penne for about 10 minutes or until al dente (tender but firm to the bite). Drain and return to the pot. Add sauce, basil, salt and pepper; toss to coat. Transfer to a warm serving bowl and sprinkle with cheese.

Per serving 620 calories, 18 g protein, 18 g fat, 86 g carbohydrates, 6 g fiber

Penne with Devil Sauce

Penne Rigate alla Diavola

2 tbsp (25 mL) extra-virgin olive oil
6 cloves garlic, minced
2 tsp (10 mL) anchovy paste
½ tsp (2 mL) hot pepper flakes
1 can (28 oz/796 mL) diced tomatoes
1 jar (12 oz/340 mL) roasted red bell
  peppers, drained and thinly sliced

1 lb (500 g) penne rigate
¼ cup (50 mL) chopped pitted oil-
  cured black olives (optional)
1 tbsp (15 mL) chopped fresh
  oregano or marjoram

In a large skillet, heat oil over medium heat. Add garlic, anchovy paste and hot pepper flakes; cook, stirring, for 2 minutes or until garlic is starting to turn golden. Add tomatoes and roasted red peppers; bring to a boil. Reduce heat and simmer, uncovered, for 15 minutes or until thickened.

Meanwhile, in a large pot of boiling salted water, cook penne for about 10 minutes or until al dente (tender but firm to the bite). Drain and return to the pot. Add sauce, olives (if using) and oregano; toss to coat.

Per serving 500 calories, 16 g protein, 9 g fat, 89 g carbohydrates, 7 g fiber

Penne with Mushrooms and Peppers

Penne con Funghi e Peperoni

Makes 4 servings

Mushrooms and peppers work so well together, and they make a perfect sauce for pasta. Chunky sauces go well with short pasta—it's much easier to get both sauce and pasta on the fork! Try this sauce with rigatoni; the mushrooms and peppers often sneak into the hole in the pasta for a surprise in each bite.

Tip

For 1 lb (500 g) penne, you will need 6 cups (1.5 L) dried pasta.

¼ cup (50 mL) extra-virgin olive oil
4 cloves garlic, minced
2 red bell peppers, thinly sliced
8 oz (250 g) mushrooms, sliced
½ tsp (2 mL) hot pepper flakes

1 lb (500 g) penne rigate
¼ cup (50 mL) chopped fresh
  Italian parsley
1 tsp (5 mL) salt

In a large nonstick skillet, heat oil over medium-high heat. Add garlic, red peppers, mushrooms and hot pepper flakes; cook, stirring, for about 10 minutes or until mushrooms are golden brown and no liquid remains.

Meanwhile, in a large pot of boiling salted water, cook penne for about 10 minutes or until al dente (tender but firm to the bite). Drain, reserving 1 cup (250 mL) of the cooking water, and return pasta to the pot. Add mushroom mixture, parsley and salt; toss to combine. Add enough of the reserved pasta cooking water to moisten.

VARIATION

Add 8 oz (250 g) sausage, cooked and sliced, to the mushroom mixture before tossing it with the pasta.

Per serving 530 calories, 15 g protein, 16 g fat, 81 g carbohydrates, 5 g fiber

Beef Ravioli with Quick Sauce

Ravioli di Manzo con Salsa Rapida

2 tbsp (25 mL) extra-virgin olive oil
2 cloves garlic, minced
1 small onion, finely chopped
2 chicken or turkey sausages, casings removed
1 jar (23 oz/660 mL) tomato passata
½ cup (125 mL) water
1 tsp (5 mL) salt
½ tsp (2 mL) dried oregano
6 basil leaves
1 lb (500 g) beef or chicken ravioli
¼ cup (50 mL) freshly grated Parmigiano-Reggiano cheese

In a medium saucepan, heat half of the oil over medium heat. Add garlic and onion; cook, stirring, for 3 minutes or until softened.

Crumble sausage into saucepan; cook, breaking up with the back of a spoon, for about 8 minutes or until no longer pink. Add passata, water, salt and oregano; bring to a boil. Add basil and reduce heat. Simmer, uncovered, for about 20 minutes or until thickened. Add the remaining oil.

Meanwhile, in a large pot of boiling salted water, cook ravioli for about 6 minutes or until they float to the top and are tender. Drain and return to the pot. Add sauce and toss to coat. Transfer to a warm serving bowl and sprinkle with cheese.

Makes 4 servings

While I was staying in Italy, I needed some quick dinners to feed my family, and this is one that everyone loved. I whipped up the sauce quickly with the help of the tomato passata. A plain passata works well, but try one flavored with basil or another herb.

Tips

Tomato passata (tomato purée) comes in tall, thin glass jars. You can find it in most grocery stores.

Fresh and frozen ravioli work equally well.

For 1 lb (500 g) ravioli, you will need 3 cups (750 mL).

Per serving 470 calories, 21 g protein, 18 g fat, 55 g carbohydrates, 6 g fiber

Bruschetta Ravioli

Ravioli alla Bruschetta

Makes 3 to 4 servings

Bruschetta is a tomato mixture usually used as a topping for crusty bread; here, it makes a light pasta sauce. Look for a cheese-filled pasta or one filled with spinach and ricotta.

Tip

For 12 oz (350 g) ravioli, you will need 2½ cups (625 mL).

2 tbsp (25 mL) extra-virgin olive oil	Pinch hot pepper flakes
4 plum tomatoes, diced	¼ tsp (1 mL) salt
2 cloves garlic, minced	12 oz (350 g) cheese ravioli
1 tbsp (15 mL) chopped fresh	or agnolotti
Italian parsley	¼ cup (50 mL) freshly grated
½ tsp (2 mL) dried oregano	Parmigiano-Reggiano cheese

In a large nonstick skillet, heat oil over medium heat. Add tomatoes and garlic; cook, stirring, for about 4 minutes or until becoming saucy. Add parsley, oregano and hot pepper flakes; cook, stirring occasionally, for about 8 minutes or until sauce thickens slightly. Add salt.

Meanwhile, in a large pot of boiling salted water, cook ravioli for about 6 minutes or until they float to the top and are tender. Drain, add to skillet and toss to coat. Transfer to a warm serving bowl and sprinkle with cheese.

Per each of 4 servings 320 calories, 13 g protein, 16 g fat, 32 g carbohydrates, 3 g fiber

Gorgonzola Walnut Gnocchi

Gnocchi con Noci e Gorgonzola

3 tbsp (45 mL) butter
½ cup (125 mL) finely chopped
  walnuts
1 cup (250 mL) light (5%) cream
4 oz (125 g) Gorgonzola cheese

2 tbsp (25 mL) chopped fresh Italian
  parsley
¼ tsp (1 mL) freshly ground black
  pepper
1 lb (500 g) potato gnocchi

Makes 4 servings

I love cream sauces, but I know you shouldn't eat them all the time. I splurge about once a week. With Gorgonzola cheese, this one is doubly rich.

In a large nonstick skillet, melt butter over medium heat until foamy. Add walnuts and cook, stirring, for 30 seconds. Add cream and bring to a boil. Slowly stir in Gorgonzola; reduce heat and simmer, uncovered, for about 5 minutes or until thickened and smooth. Stir in parsley and pepper.

Meanwhile, in a large pot of boiling salted water, cook gnocchi for about 5 minutes or until they float to the top and are tender. Drain, add to skillet and toss to coat. Cook over low heat for 2 minutes.

Tips

Try toasting the walnuts: it will increase the nutty flavor of the sauce. To toast nuts, spread them on a baking sheet and toast in a 350°F (180°C) oven for 7 to 8 minutes, or until lightly browned.

Either fresh or frozen gnocchi will work well. You can also use homemade spinach ricotta gnocchi (see recipe, page 21) if you have the time.

For perfectly cooked gnocchi, add it to the boiling water when you add the Gorgonzola to the sauce—they'll be done at the same time.

For 1 lb (500 g) gnocchi, you will need 3 cups (750 mL).

Per serving 590 calories, 15 g protein, 47 g fat, 27 g carbohydrates, 2 g fiber

Spinach Ricotta Cappelletti

Cappelletti Ripieni di Spinaci e Ricotta

Makes 4 servings

Cappelletti look like little hats and are interchangeable with tortellini. Other fillings, such as mushroom, chicken or beef, are also great with this sauce.

Tips

For 1 lb (500 g) cappelletti, you will need 4 cups (1 L).

1 cup (250 mL) whipping (35%) cream
2 small cloves garlic, minced
¼ tsp (1 mL) freshly ground black pepper

1 lb (500 g) spinach ricotta cappelletti
3 tbsp (45 mL) freshly grated Parmigiano-Reggiano cheese

In a large skillet, bring whipping cream to a boil over medium heat. Add garlic and pepper; boil for 2 minutes.

Meanwhile, in a large pot of boiling salted water, cook cappelletti for about 6 minutes or until they float to the top and are tender. Drain, add to sauce and toss to coat. Transfer to a warm serving bowl and sprinkle with cheese.

VARIATIONS

Rosé Sauce: Add ½ cup (125 mL) pasta sauce to the whipping cream.

Mushroom Sauce: Sauté 8 oz (250 g) mushrooms, sliced, in 1 tbsp (15 mL) butter with a pinch of salt and pepper and add to sauce with cappelletti.

Per serving 510 calories, 16 g protein, 31 g fat, 41 g carbohydrates, 2 g fiber

Pasta with Peas

Pasta ai Piselli

12 oz (375 g) orecchiette or small
  shell pasta
1 large Yukon gold potato, peeled
  and diced (about 6 oz/175 g)
2 tbsp (25 mL) extra-virgin olive oil
2 cloves garlic, minced
1 small onion, finely chopped
¾ tsp (4 mL) dried oregano
¼ tsp (1 mL) hot pepper flakes
2 cups (500 mL) frozen peas

¼ cup (50 mL) vegetable stock
  (store-bought or see recipe,
  page 22) or water
2 tbsp (50 mL) chopped fresh Italian
  parsley
¼ tsp (1 mL) salt
Pinch freshly ground black pepper
¼ cup (50 mL) freshly grated
  Parmigiano-Reggiano cheese

Makes 4 servings

Here is a pasta dish in
which shape really
does matter. Pasta
with a cup shape, such
as orecchiette or
shells, is perfect for
holding the peas.

Tip

For 12 oz (375 g) orecchiette
or shells, you will need 4 cups
(1 L) dried pasta.

In a large pot of boiling salted water, cook orecchiette and potato for about
10 minutes or until pasta is al dente (tender but firm to the bite) and potato
is tender. Drain, reserving 1 cup (250 mL) of the cooking water, and return
pasta and potato to the pot.

Meanwhile, in a large nonstick skillet, heat oil over medium heat. Add garlic, onion, oregano and hot pepper flakes; cook, stirring, for 3 minutes or
until softened. Add peas, stock, parsley, salt and pepper; bring to a simmer.
Cover and simmer for 5 minutes to allow flavors to blend. Pour over pasta
and toss to coat. Sprinkle with cheese and add enough of the reserved water
to moisten.

VARIATION

For a heartier meal, add 1 cup (250 mL) chopped ham with peas.

Per serving 540 calories, 19 g protein, 11 g fat, 90 g carbohydrates, 8 g fiber

long pasta

I remember trying for hours as a child to twist my spaghetti onto my fork like the big kids did. There was a lot of slurping, and many tablecloths became laden with tomato sauce while I practiced. I would get so frustrated—and then one day I just got it. Now it's my son's turn to try. Thinking I was being smart, I gave him his spaghetti with butter instead of tomato sauce . . . sure enough, that makes a mess too.

No matter what the sauce is, long pasta is a true kid favorite. Long pastas are terrific with rich tomato sauces, but also hold up to the bold bite of a garlic-and-oil sauce. As with short pasta, there's tons of variety—everything from thick, flat noodles like fettuccine (little ribbons) to thin, delicate noodles like cappelli di angeli (angel hair). I still think spaghetti will win out with most kids, just because it's fun to say "pasghetti."

Butter Pasta

Pasta al Burro

Makes 4 servings

I grew up on this simple recipe, and now my son is too! It's so easy and tasty and cheap that it's perfect for a university student. No butter? No problem: drizzle some olive oil over top. If you have leftovers, add them to a frittata the next night.

Tip

To make this dish especially sweet and creamy, I add a bit more butter. My son, who eats butter like cheese, really appreciates it!

1 lb (500 g) spaghetti or spaghettini
¼ cup (50 mL) freshly grated
  Parmigiano-Reggiano cheese

¼ cup (50 mL) butter

In a large pot of boiling salted water, cook spaghetti for 8 to 10 minutes or until al dente (tender but firm to the bite). Drain and return to the pot. Stir in cheese and butter until well combined.

Per serving 580 calories, 18 g protein, 16 g fat, 90 g carbohydrates, 5 g fiber

Brunella's Awesome and Easy Pasta

Pasta Semplice di Brunella

12 oz (375 g) spinach linguine
⅓ cup (75 mL) extra-virgin olive oil
2 tbsp (25 mL) roasted garlic and
  pepper seasoning mix

¼ cup (50 mL) freshly grated
  Parmigiano-Reggiano cheese

In a large pot of boiling salted water, cook linguine for 8 to 10 minutes or until al dente (tender but firm to the bite). Drain and return to the pot.

Meanwhile, in a nonstick skillet, heat oil over low heat. Add seasoning mix and cook, stirring, for 30 seconds or until fragrant. Pour over spaghetti and toss to coat. Transfer to a warm serving bowl and sprinkle with cheese.

Makes 3 servings

My cousin Brunella served this dish to my husband and me, to rave reviews. He asked for thirds, and I followed suit. Her secret ingredient? The roasted garlic and pepper seasoning mix.

Tip
Look for roasted garlic and pepper seasoning mix in the spice aisle.

Per serving 580 calories, 15 g protein, 29 g fat, 65 g carbohydrates, 3 g fiber

Rapini Pasta with Garlic Bread Crumbs

Pasta e Rapini con Pane ed Aglio

Makes 4 servings

Rapini is a dark green leafy vegetable that is often tossed into a pasta sauce or risotto. It is also delicious on its own. Here, it is matched with spaghetti; the added texture of the bread crumbs makes it a surefire winner at my house.

Tip

For a simple side dish, cook the rapini and bread crumb mixture and serve without pasta.

1 bunch rapini	½ tsp (2 mL) salt
1 cup (250 mL) water	Pinch freshly ground black pepper
½ cup (125 mL) extra-virgin olive oil	12 oz (375 g) spaghetti
3 cloves garlic, minced	3 tbsp (45 mL) freshly grated
¾ cup (175 mL) fresh bread crumbs	Parmigiano-Reggiano cheese

Trim 1 inch (2.5 cm) off ends of rapini and discard. Chop the remaining rapini coarsely. In a large nonstick skillet, heat water over medium-high heat. Add rapini in a single layer, in batches if necessary; cover and steam for about 5 minutes or until tender. Drain well and set aside. (*Rapini can be cooked up to 2 days ahead. Store in an airtight container in the refrigerator.*)

In the same skillet, heat oil over medium-high heat. Add garlic and bread crumbs; cook, stirring, for about 1 minute or until garlic is golden. Add rapini, salt and pepper; cook, stirring, for 2 minutes or until heated through.

Meanwhile, in a large pot of boiling salted water, cook spaghetti for 8 to 10 minutes or until al dente (tender but firm to the bite). Drain, reserving ½ cup (125 mL) of the cooking water, and return spaghetti to the pot. Add rapini sauce and enough of the reserved water to moisten; toss to combine. Transfer to a warm serving bowl and sprinkle with cheese.

VARIATIONS

Substitute penne rigate or orecchiette for the spaghetti.

Substitute spinach for the rapini.

Per serving 660 calories, 17 g protein, 32 g fat, 77 g carbohydrates, 4 g fiber

Spaghetti Carbonara

Pasta alla Carbonara

12 oz (375 g) spaghetti
6 slices pancetta
4 eggs
⅓ cup (75 mL) freshly grated
  Parmigiano-Reggiano or
  Romano cheese

¼ cup (50 mL) chopped fresh Italian
  parsley
Pinch freshly ground black pepper

Makes 4 servings

Why go out to a
restaurant for good
pasta when it's so easy
to prepare and enjoy
at home?

In a large pot of boiling salted water, cook spaghetti for 8 to 10 minutes or until al dente (tender but firm to the bite). Drain and return to the pot. Keep warm over medium heat.

Meanwhile, in a skillet, cook pancetta over medium-low heat for about 5 minutes or until slightly crisp. Drain on plate lined with paper towels. Chop and set aside.

In a medium bowl, using a fork, beat together eggs, cheese, parsley and pepper. Immediately pour into pasta; cook, tossing, for about 30 seconds or until eggs are lightly cooked and pasta is well coated. Add pancetta and toss to combine.

VARIATIONS
For extra color and nutrition, add 1 cup (250 mL) cooked chopped vegetables, such as broccoli, roasted red peppers, asparagus or zucchini to the pasta.

For a smoky taste, substitute bacon for the pancetta.

Per serving 510 calories, 26 g protein, 16 g fat, 65 g carbohydrates, 2 g fiber

Spaghetti with Pancetta and Parmesan

Pasta con Pancetta e Parmigiano

Makes 4 servings

Come home to real and rustic cuisine. The simple flavors of pasta, pancetta and cheese produce a memorable dish that's quick enough to make on a weeknight.

Tip

Try other pastas, such as linguine, bucatini, tagliatelle or penne, instead of spaghetti.

1 tbsp (15 mL) extra-virgin olive oil	12 oz (375 g) spaghetti
4 oz (125 g) pancetta or bacon, diced	1/3 cup (75 mL) freshly grated
4 cloves garlic, minced	Parmigiano-Reggiano or
1 onion, finely chopped	Romano cheese
1/4 tsp (1 mL) hot pepper flakes	1/4 cup (50 mL) chopped fresh
1 can (28 oz/796 mL) tomatoes	Italian parsley

In a large skillet, heat oil over medium heat. Add pancetta and cook, stirring for 5 minutes or until crisp. Add garlic and onion; cook, stirring, for 5 minutes or until softened. Add hot pepper flakes and stir to coat. Stir in tomatoes, breaking up with the back of a spoon; boil gently, uncovered, for about 15 minutes or until thickened.

Meanwhile, in a large pot of boiling salted water, cook spaghetti for 8 to 10 minutes or until al dente (tender but firm to the bite). Drain and return to the pot. Add sauce and stir to coat. Stir in half each of the cheese and parsley. Transfer to a warm serving bowl and sprinkle with the remaining cheese and parsley.

Per serving 560 calories, 24 g protein, 17 g fat, 77 g carbohydrates, 5 g fiber

Garlic Shrimp and Olive Oil Linguine

Linguine con Gamberi, Aglio e Olio d'oliva

1/4 cup (50 mL) extra-virgin olive oil
8 cloves garlic, minced
1/4 tsp (1 mL) hot pepper flakes
1 lb (500 g) large raw shrimp, peeled
  and deveined

1/2 cup (125 mL) chopped fresh Italian
  parsley
1/2 cup (125 mL) dry white wine
Pinch salt
1 pkg (12 oz/350 g) fresh linguine

Makes 4 servings

This recipe is fast enough for a week-night meal, but elegant enough for company.

Tips

For really quick dinners, look for fresh pasta in the grocery store. Because it is fresh, it cooks in half the time it takes dried pasta. If you want to use dried pasta, add 5 minutes to the cooking time.

If you don't have white wine, use an equal amount of vegetable or chicken stock and a splash of white wine vinegar.

In a large nonstick skillet, heat oil over medium-low heat. Add garlic and hot pepper flakes; cook, stirring, for 2 minutes or until garlic is softened and beginning to turn golden. Increase heat to medium-high; add shrimp and cook for 2 minutes. Add half of the parsley, the wine and salt; boil for 2 minutes or until shrimp are pink and opaque.

Meanwhile, in a large pot of boiling salted water, cook linguine for about 5 minutes or until al dente (tender but firm to the bite). Drain and return to the pot. Add shrimp mixture and the remaining parsley; toss to combine.

VARIATIONS
Substitute large sea scallops for the shrimp.

Use fettuccine or spaghetti instead of linguine, if you prefer.

Per serving 510 calories, 33 g protein, 18 g fat, 50 g carbohydrates, 4 g fiber

Linguine with Ricotta

Linguine con Ricotta

Makes 4 servings

Linguine, which means "little tongues," is perfect for this rich cheese sauce. Like most pasta dishes, this one does not wait—when it's ready, you should be too! Serve it right away and make sure everyone is at the table with forks in hand.

Tips

If you have frozen vegetables, such as peas, simply warm them in the microwave and toss them into the pasta.

For a smoother sauce, use extra-smooth ricotta.

1 lb (500 g) linguine
1 tub (16 oz/454 g) ricotta cheese
2 tbsp (25 mL) extra-virgin olive oil

2 tbsp (25 mL) chopped fresh Italian parsley
Pinch salt
Pinch hot pepper flakes (optional)

In a large pot of boiling salted water, cook linguine for 8 to 10 minutes or until al dente (tender but firm to the bite). Drain, reserving 1 cup (250 mL) of the cooking water, and return linguine to the pot. Add ricotta, oil and enough of the reserved water to moisten; toss until a smooth sauce forms. Add parsley, salt and hot pepper flakes, if using; toss to combine.

Per serving 600 calories, 26 g protein, 24 g fat, 69 g carbohydrates, 3 g fiber

Oil and Garlic Pasta

Linguine all'Aglio ed Olio

1 lb (500 g) linguine
⅓ cup (75 mL) extra-virgin olive oil
4 cloves garlic, minced

¼ cup (50 mL) freshly grated
  Parmigiano-Reggiano or
  Romano cheese
2 tbsp (25 mL) chopped fresh
  Italian parsley

In a large pot of boiling salted water, cook linguine for 8 to 10 minutes or until al dente (tender but firm to the bite). Drain and return to the pot.

Meanwhile, in a nonstick skillet, heat oil over medium-low heat. Add garlic and cook, stirring, for about 2 minutes or until softened but not golden. Pour over linguine and toss to coat. Add cheese and parsley; toss to combine.

Makes 4 servings

Most people use spaghetti in this dish, but I enjoy linguine with the garlic and oil. This recipe can have as much flavor as you like: by adding more garlic, you'll increase your chances of getting an Italian over for dinner!

Tips

If you want to spice this recipe up a bit, add ¼ tsp (1 mL) hot pepper flakes with the oil and garlic.

For a subtle garlic flavor, cut the garlic into slivers and add to oil. You can remove the garlic slivers before tossing the sauce with the pasta.

Per serving 520 calories, 14 g protein, 23 g fat, 65 g carbohydrates, 3 g fiber

Linguine with Puttanesca Sauce

Linguine alla Puttanesca

Makes 2 to 3 servings

When Chef Michael Mandato, executive chef at Fairmont Jasper Park Lodge, decided to redo the restaurant's menus, he wanted to add a splash of Italian cuisine to the Meadows dining room. He decided on this classic, pungent dish and added a seafood twist. Puttanesca gets its name from Italian ladies of the evening, who wanted to work, but still had to put dinner on the table for their families. The recipe needed to be fast but taste like it had been cooking all day. This sure did the trick . . .

½ cup (125 mL) extra-virgin olive oil
15 sea scallops
10 large raw shrimp, peeled and deveined
¼ tsp (1 mL) salt
¼ tsp (1 mL) freshly ground black pepper
½ tsp (2 mL) anchovy paste
2 cloves garlic, minced
1 onion, finely diced
3 cups (750 mL) diced plum tomatoes

1 tbsp (15 mL) tomato paste
2 tbsp (25 mL) chopped pitted oil-cured black olives
1 tbsp (15 mL) capers
1 tbsp (15 mL) minced fresh basil
1 tbsp (15 mL) minced fresh thyme
1 tbsp (15 mL) minced fresh Italian parsley
1 tbsp (15 mL) minced fresh oregano
8 oz (250 g) linguine
¼ cup (50 mL) freshly grated Parmigiano-Reggiano cheese

In a medium saucepan, heat 2 tbsp (25 mL) of the oil over medium-high heat. Add scallops, shrimp and a pinch each of salt and pepper; cook, stirring, for about 2 minutes or until scallops are light golden and shrimp are pink. Remove to a plate and keep warm.

Add 2 tbsp (25 mL) of the oil to the pan and cook anchovy paste for 30 seconds or until dissolved. Add garlic and onion; cook, stirring, for 3 minutes or until softened. Add tomatoes and the remaining salt and pepper; simmer for about 8 minutes or until tomatoes are soft. Add tomato paste and cook for 5 minutes. Stir in scallops, shrimp, olives, capers and half each of the basil, thyme, parsley and oregano.

Meanwhile, in a large pot of boiling salted water, cook linguine for about 8 to 10 minutes or until al dente (tender but firm to the bite). Drain, return to the pot and toss with the remaining oil, basil, thyme, parsley and oregano. Scrape into a large serving bowl, top with tomato sauce and sprinkle with cheese.

VARIATION

Fresh Herbs: If all the fresh herbs are not available use all of one, such as ¼ cup (50 mL) of fresh basil or Italian parsley or a combination of two. Try 2 tbsp (25mL) each of thyme and oregano. All options will work well, although ¼ cup (50 mL) of thyme would be a little potent for this sauce.

Tips

If you can't find anchovy paste, you can substitute 1 anchovy fillet, minced.

Use drained canned diced tomatoes instead of dicing fresh tomatoes yourself.

Per each of 3 servings 750 calories, 31 g protein, 43 g fat, 59 g carbohydrates, 6 g fiber

Linguine with Easy Gorgonzola Cheese Sauce

Linguine con Salsa Facile di Gorgonzola

Makes 4 servings

This creamy, rich white sauce, which coats tagliatelle, fettuccine and even gnocchi perfectly manages to be both simple and decadent.

1 lb (500 g) linguine
2 tbsp (25mL) butter
1 small shallot, diced
1½ cups (375 mL) whipping (35%) cream

4 oz (125 g) Gorgonzola or blue cheese, crumbled
Pinch freshly ground black pepper
2 tbsp (25 mL) freshly grated Parmigiano-Reggiano cheese

In a large pot of boiling salted water, cook linguine for 8 to 10 minutes or until al dente (tender but firm to the bite). Drain and return to the pot. In a large skillet, melt butter over medium heat. Sauté shallot for 3 minutes or until softened. Add cream and bring to a boil for about 5 minutes or until reduced slightly. Reduce heat and stir in Gorgonzola and pepper until melted and thickened. Toss with cooked pasta. Sprinkle with Parmigiano-Reggiano cheese; toss again. Serve immeditaely.

Per serving 850 calories, 22 g protein, 50 g fat, 78 g carbohydrates, 3 g fiber

Springtime Fettuccine with Tomatoes

Fettuccine Primavera con Pomodori

2 tbsp (25 mL) extra-virgin olive oil
4 cloves garlic, minced
¼ tsp (1 mL) hot pepper flakes
1 red bell pepper, thinly sliced
1 zucchini, cut in half lengthwise and
  thinly sliced (about 4 oz/125 g)
2 cups (500 mL) chopped fresh
  asparagus or fresh or frozen peas
¼ tsp (1 mL) salt
Pinch freshly ground black pepper

1 cup (250 mL) pasta sauce (store-
  bought or see recipe, page 20)
1 cup (250 mL) vegetable stock
  (store-bought or see recipe, page
  22)
12 oz (375 g) fettuccine or linguine
¼ cup (50 mL) chopped fresh Italian
  parsley
2 tbsp (25 mL) freshly grated
  Parmigiano-Reggiano cheese

Makes 4 servings

Primavera means
"springtime," but
don't let that limit you
to spring vegetables.
Other vegetables,
such as broccoli and
cauliflower, work well
in this dish too.

In a large saucepan, heat oil over medium heat. Add garlic and hot pepper flakes; cook, stirring, for 1 minute. Add red pepper, zucchini, asparagus, salt and black pepper; cook, stirring, for about 5 minutes or until vegetables are tender-crisp. Add pasta sauce and stock; bring to a boil. Reduce heat, and simmer for 10 minutes.

Meanwhile, in a large pot of boiling salted water, cook fettuccine for about 10 minutes or until al dente (tender but firm to the bite). Drain and return to the pot. Add sauce, parsley and cheese; toss to coat.

VARIATIONS

In late summer or early fall, substitute 2 cups (500 mL) chopped fresh plum tomatoes for the pasta sauce for a real hit of fresh tomato flavor.

To add some kick, chop a fresh hot pepper, such as a finger chili or jalapeño, and cook it with the vegetables—that's a spicy pasta!

Per serving 400 calories, 14 g protein, 11 g fat, 62 g carbohydrates, 7 g fiber

Mushroom Fettuccine Alfredo

Fettuccine Alfredo con Funghi

Makes 4 servings

I adore fettuccine Alfredo and can never get enough, but I do like to change it up a bit from time to time, adding different vegetables and sometimes prosciutto and fresh herbs.

Tips

Try to time this recipe so that the pasta is ready right when the sauce has thickened. Toss them together at the table for a dramatic presentation.

To deepen the flavor, try using wild mushrooms such as chanterelles in the sauce.

For a richer sauce, use whipping (35%) cream instead of half-and-half.

1 tbsp (15 mL) butter
8 oz (250 g) sliced mushrooms
¼ tsp (1 mL) dried thyme
½ tsp (2 mL) salt
¼ tsp (1 mL) freshly ground black pepper
1½ cups (375 mL) half-and-half (10%) cream

½ cup (125 mL) freshly grated Parmigiano-Reggiano or Romano cheese
1 lb (500 g) fresh fettuccine or tagliatelle
2 tbsp (25 mL) chopped fresh basil or Italian parsley

In a large nonstick skillet, melt butter over medium-high heat. Add mushrooms, thyme, salt and pepper; cook, stirring, for about 8 minutes or until mushrooms are golden. Add cream and cheese; bring to a boil. Reduce heat and simmer, uncovered, for about 8 minutes or until thickened.

Meanwhile, in a large pot of boiling salted water, cook fettuccine for about 5 minutes or until al dente (tender but firm to the bite). Drain and pour into a large deep platter. Add sauce and toss to coat. Sprinkle with basil.

Per serving 540 calories, 22 g protein, 20 g fat, 69 g carbohydrates, 5 g fiber

Seafood Pasta

Spaghetti Cozze e Vongole

1 tbsp (15 mL) extra-virgin olive oil
3 cloves garlic, minced
4 plum tomatoes, seeded and
  chopped
2 tbsp (25 mL) chopped fresh basil
¼ tsp (1 mL) salt

¼ tsp (1 mL) freshly ground black
  pepper
8 oz (250 g) small clams, scrubbed
8 oz (250 g) mussels, rinsed
½ cup (125 mL) dry white wine
8 oz (250 g) spaghetti

In a large deep skillet, heat oil over medium heat. Add garlic and cook, stirring, for 1 minute or until softened. Add tomatoes, basil, salt and pepper; reduce heat and simmer, uncovered, for 5 minutes. Stir in clams, mussels and wine; cover and simmer for 8 minutes or until clams and mussels open.

Meanwhile, in a large pot of boiling salted water, cook spaghetti for 8 to 10 minutes or until al dente (tender but firm to the bite). Drain and add to sauce; toss to combine.

Makes 2 servings

The night we arrived in Italy, this dish really hit the spot. Being close to the water sometimes makes you crave seafood, but you can enjoy it even when you're not seaside. For the freshest flavor, this recipe is best made when tomatoes are in season.

Tip

Check clams and mussels before adding them to the sauce. The shells should be tightly closed. If a shell is slightly open, give it a little tap; if it doesn't close, discard it. Once they are cooked, discard any that have not opened. This gives you two chances to get rid of the bad ones.

Per serving 760 calories, 47 g protein, 13 g fat, 104 g carbohydrates, 7 g fiber

Spinach Ricotta Cannelloni

Cannelloni Ripieni con Spinaci e Ricotta

Makes 6 to 8 servings

Making your own pasta can be a time-consuming process, but with store-bought fresh pasta this dish becomes easy enough for a weeknight meal. Make sure there's bread on the table to sop up any leftover sauce!

1 pkg (350 g) fresh pasta sheets
2 eggs, lightly beaten
1 pkg (10 oz/300 g) fresh spinach, cooked, drained and chopped
1 tub (16 oz/454 g) ricotta cheese
1 cup (250 mL) shredded mozzarella cheese
½ cup (125 mL) freshly grated Parmigiano-Reggiano cheese
⅓ cup (75 mL) chopped fresh Italian parsley
Pinch salt
Pinch freshly ground black pepper
4 cups (1 L) pasta sauce (store-bought or see recipe, page 20)

In a large pot of boiling salted water, cook pasta, 2 sheets at a time, for about 2 minutes or until softened. Remove from water and lay flat on a damp tea towel. Repeat with the remaining pasta. Cut each sheet in half crosswise.

Meanwhile, in a large bowl, stir together eggs, spinach, ricotta, mozzarella, ⅓ cup (75 mL) of the Parmigiano-Reggiano, half of the parsley, salt and pepper.

Place about 3 tbsp (45 mL) of the filling in the center of each piece of pasta and roll up into a cylinder. Repeat with the remaining filling and pasta. (*Place in an airtight container and store overnight in the refrigerator or in the freezer for up to 1 month. Add 15 minutes to the baking time if cooking cold cannelloni.*)

Spread 1½ cups (375 mL) of the pasta sauce evenly in the bottom of a 13- x 9-inch (3 L) baking dish. Place cannelloni snugly in the dish. Pour the remaining sauce over top. Sprinkle with the remaining Parmigiano-Reggiano cheese and parsley. (*Cover and refrigerate for up to 1 day.*) Cover and bake in the center of a 350°F (180°C) oven for about 30 minutes or until bubbly and heated through.

VARIATION

Meat and Ricotta: Omit spinach and add 8 oz (250 g) cooked lean ground veal or beef to the ricotta filling.

SHREDDING MOZZARELLA CHEESE

Cheese can be cumbersome because sometimes it seems too soft. Here's a little trick: place your cheese in the freezer for a bit to firm up before shredding. If you use a lot of shredded cheese for pastas and pizzas, shred extra and freeze it for a later dinner.

Tips

Each pasta sheet makes two cannelloni. If you don't need all the filled cannelloni, freeze the rest for another night.

For even faster cannelloni, use egg roll wrappers. They don't need to be precooked at all—just fill, roll up and bake.

If you heat up the sauce first, the cannelloni will take only about 20 minutes to heat through.

Use frozen spinach leaves instead of the fresh. Thaw and squeeze dry before using.

Cook spinach with water clinging to leaves in a non-stick skillet over medium heat for about 5 minutes or until bright green and wilted. Drain well and then squeeze out any excess water. Chop and it's ready to use.

Per each of 8 servings 410 calories, 22 g protein, 17 g fat, 41 g carbohydrates, 6 g fiber

eggs and vegetarian

Eggs aren't just for breakfast and baking anymore: they are more popular than ever for dinner. Eggs are an important staple in most Italian homes. I can't do without them in my house, as I like to eat frittatas on a regular basis. Everyone has some in their fridge—why not be creative and whip up eggs in tomato sauce or a frittata to fill those hungry tummies?

Although many of the dishes throughout the book are vegetarian, the ones in this chapter were created specifically with vegetarians in mind. Nana, who is not a vegetarian but enjoys making vegetarian dishes, introduced me to Potato-Stuffed Zucchini (page 112), which is creamy, tender and, of course, very tasty.

Dishes rich in vegetables and eggs are lighter, but are still filling. And they're an easy fix when you're cooking just for yourself.

Rapini Frittata

Frittata di Rape

I love rapini because of its slightly bitter and mustardy flavor. This versatile frittata is spectacular cut and placed in a crusty bun for a dinner sandwich. Or try it with a little pasta sauce on top. Enjoy it hot or cold with a side salad, or serve it up in little squares as an appetizer.

1 bunch rapini, trimmed	¼ tsp (1 mL) freshly ground black
2 tbsp (25 mL) extra-virgin olive oil	pepper
2 cloves garlic, minced	6 eggs
¼ tsp (1 mL) hot pepper flakes	¼ cup (50 mL) freshly grated
½ tsp (2 mL) salt	Parmigiano-Reggiano cheese

In a large pot of boiling water, cook rapini for about 6 minutes or until tender. Drain well and, with a wooden spatula, gently push down on rapini to squeeze out as much water as possible. Chop coarsely.

In a large nonstick skillet, heat oil over medium heat. Add garlic and hot pepper flakes; cook, stirring, for 1 minute or until fragrant. Add rapini and half of the salt and toss to coat; cook, stirring, for about 8 minutes or until starting to brown and become crispy.

In a large bowl, whisk together eggs, cheese, remaining salt and black pepper. Pour into skillet, stirring to combine. Cook, lifting edges with a rubber spatula to let runny egg go to the bottom, until bottom is light golden and top is set. Place a large plate over the skillet and invert frittata onto plate. Slide frittata back into the skillet and cook for about 3 minutes or until bottom is golden.

Per serving 230 calories, 15 g protein, 16 g fat, 6 g carbohydrates, 0 g fiber

Asparagus Frittata

Frittata d'Asparagi

1½ cups (375 mL) water
2 cups (500 mL) chopped fresh
　asparagus
½ tsp (2 mL) salt
¼ tsp (1 mL) freshly ground black
　pepper

1 cup (250 mL) all-purpose flour
2 tsp (10 mL) baking powder
1 egg
2 tbsp (25 mL) chopped fresh basil
¼ cup (50 mL) vegetable oil or extra-
　virgin olive oil

Makes 2 to 3 servings

Frittatas are flat-cooked skillet pancakes that may or may not have eggs. This frittata is heavier than traditional egg frittatas, but it helps that it has an egg. It takes practice to master this recipe. It's all about stirring the flour mixture properly to create a light frittata rather than a heavy pancake. It may take a couple tries, as it did for me, but it's worth it. If, in the end, it doesn't work out, you can call my aunt and she'll come over and make it for you. I use an 8-inch skillet for this recipe.

In a medium nonstick skillet, bring ½ cup (125 mL) of the water to a boil. Add asparagus, cover and cook for 3 minutes or until tender. Drain and rinse under cold water. Drain well and toss with a pinch each of salt and pepper; set aside.

In a medium bowl, whisk together flour, baking powder, and the remaining salt and pepper. Add the remaining water and egg; whisk to form a smooth batter. Add basil and stir to distribute evenly.

In the same skillet, heat half of the oil over medium-low heat. Pour in batter and sprinkle with asparagus. Using a fork, gently fold asparagus into the batter to form a thick paste; cook, stirring and folding, until batter thickens. Pat into a flat frittata and cook for about 15 minutes or until bottom is golden brown. Place a large plate over the skillet and invert frittata onto plate. Add remaining oil to the skillet and slide frittata back in; cook for 10 minutes or until bottom is light golden.

VARIATION
Add ½ cup (125 mL) chopped ham with the asparagus.

Per each of 3 servings 370 calories, 9 g protein, 21 g fat, 37 g carbohydrates, 3 g fiber

Friday Frittata

Frittata per Venerdi

Makes 4 servings

When I think of someone who loves to cook and enjoys life, I think of Elizabeth Baird. She has shared many ideas and good times with me. I consider her an honorary Italian because she enjoys my food so much! With her busy schedule, she is a master of putting things together fast, and frittatas are one of her favorite foods. This is one that comes to the rescue, especially at the end of the week. Vary the herbs, vegetables and cheese to suit what's left in your fridge or freezer. Add a spoonful of hot pasta sauce on top, and serve crusty bread and a green salad as accompaniments.

2 tbsp (25 mL) extra-virgin olive oil
2 Yukon gold potatoes, peeled and diced (about 8 oz/250 g total)
2 cloves garlic, slivered
1 onion, chopped
½ cup (125 mL) diced red or green bell pepper
½ tsp (2 mL) Italian herb seasoning (store-bought or see recipe, page 17)
½ tsp (2 mL) salt
¼ tsp (1 mL) freshly ground black pepper
1 cup (250 mL) frozen peas, broccoli or corn
6 eggs
1 cup (250 mL) shredded cheese, such as Cheddar, Gruyère or Gouda

In a large ovenproof skillet, heat oil over medium-high heat. Add potatoes, garlic, onion, red pepper, Italian herb seasoning, salt and black pepper; cook, stirring, for about 5 minutes or until edges of vegetables are starting to brown. Reduce heat to medium, cover and cook for about 5 minutes or until potatoes are tender. Stir in peas.

In a medium bowl, using a fork, beat eggs until frothy. Pour over potato mixture, lifting and stirring eggs into the mixture with a spatula. Cover and cook for about 8 minutes or until edges are set and puffed. Sprinkle with cheese and broil for about 2 minutes or until cheese is melted and frittata is firm.

VARIATION
Substitute ¼ cup (50 mL) freshly grated Parmigiano-Reggiano, Romano or Grana Padano for the Cheddar cheese.

Per serving 370 calories, 20 g protein, 24 g fat, 18 g carbohydrates, 4 g fiber

Zia Lina's Frittata

Frittata di Zia Lina

8 oz (250 g) spaghetti
8 eggs
¼ tsp (1 mL) salt
¼ tsp (1 mL) freshly ground black
  pepper
¾ cup (175 mL) chopped dried
  sausage packed in oil (see tip, at right)

8 oz (250 g) fresh ricotta cheese
  (see tip, at right)
¼ cup (50 mL) freshly grated
  Parmigiano-Reggiano cheese
1 tbsp (15 mL) chopped fresh basil
3 tbsp (45 mL) extra-virgin olive oil

Makes 6 servings

This frittata is hearty enough for dinner, but makes fabulous leftovers for a great breakfast! I've watched my aunt Lina make this a hundred times, and I think I might have almost perfected it.

Tips

Look for dried sausages packed in oil in mason jars at your local deli. Remove casings before chopping. You could use chorizo, kielbasa or Genoa salami, instead.

Fresh ricotta from the cheese counter is a little firmer and less watery than ricotta in tubs. In a pinch, use the tubs, but firm up ricotta before using by placing it in a sieve lined with cheesecloth and letting it sit in the refrigerator for a couple of hours.

To ovenproof your nonstick skillet with plastic handles, simply wrap with foil before placing in oven.

In a large pot of boiling salted water, cook spaghetti for 8 to 10 minutes or until al dente (tender but firm to the bite). Drain and set aside.

In a large bowl, using a fork, beat together eggs, salt and pepper. Add spaghetti and sausage; toss to coat evenly. Spoon in ricotta in large chunks and add Parmigiano-Reggiano and basil; stir gently to combine.

In a large nonstick ovenproof skillet, heat oil over medium heat. Pour in spaghetti mixture and use a fork to distribute spaghetti evenly. Cook, jiggling the pan to make sure spaghetti doesn't stick, for about 10 minutes or until almost set. Place a large plate over the skillet and invert frittata onto plate. Slide frittata back into the skillet and cook for 10 minutes or until no liquid appears when frittata is pierced with fork. (If the bottom is getting too dark, place frittata in a 250°F/120°C oven for about 5 minutes to finish cooking.)

VARIATION
Use leftover pasta tossed with sauce instead of the spaghetti. Heat up extra sauce and serve alongside.

Per serving 470 calories, 24 g protein, 28 g fat, 31 g carbohydrates, 1 g fiber

Sausage and Pepper Frittata

Frittata di Salsiccia e Peperoni

Makes 4 to 6 servings

This recipe is from my colleague and friend Maria Marotta. Her nonna Paparella would make this every couple of weeks when the fresh egg delivery came. Fifty years later, the same farmer delivers eggs to Maria's mother's home, and the farmer's son delivers eggs to Maria's house. Maria says, "Whenever I make this recipe, it reminds me of the great cooking times I had with my late nonna."

Tip

If you don't want to flip the frittata, place it in the center of a 350°F (180°C) oven after adding cheese for 10 to 12 minutes or until set. Make sure you're using an ovenproof skillet!

3 mild or hot Italian sausages, casings removed	¼ tsp (1 mL) salt
2 tbsp (25 mL) extra-virgin olive oil	¼ tsp (1 mL) freshly ground black pepper
1 red bell pepper, thinly sliced	½ cup (125 mL) shredded Asiago cheese
1 yellow bell pepper, thinly sliced	
5 eggs	

Break sausages into ½-inch (1 cm) pieces. In a large nonstick skillet, heat half of the oil over medium-high heat. Add sausages and cook, stirring, for about 5 minutes or until starting to brown. Add red and yellow peppers; cook, stirring, for about 8 minutes or until peppers are softened and sausage is no longer pink inside. Transfer to a large bowl.

In a medium bowl, using a fork, beat together eggs, salt and black pepper. Add the remaining oil to the skillet and pour in egg mixture; stir eggs gently for about 30 seconds. Add sausage mixture and stir to distribute evenly. Sprinkle with cheese and cook for about 5 minutes or until bottom is golden and top is set. Place a large plate over the skillet and invert frittata onto plate. Slide frittata back into the skillet and cook for about 3 minutes or until bottom is golden brown.

Per each of 6 servings 260 calories, 15 g protein, 20 g fat, 4 g carbohydrates, 1 g fiber

Individual Spinach and Tomato Frittatas

Frittate Piccole con Spinaci e Pomodoro

1 bag (10 oz/300 g) fresh spinach, rinsed and trimmed
¼ tsp (1 mL) salt
Pinch nutmeg
5 eggs
1½ cups (375 mL) milk
¼ cup (50 mL) freshly grated Grana Padano cheese
3 tbsp (45 mL) chopped fresh basil or Italian parsley
¼ tsp (1 mL) freshly ground black pepper
1 tomato, seeded and chopped
½ cup (125 mL) shredded Asiago, smoked provolone, fontina or Gorgonzola cheese

Makes 4 servings

Making everyone in the family his or her own frittata is so easy. These can be made ahead to reheat for dinner or for lunch the next day. Serve with some extra shredded Asiago cheese to sprinkle on top. For a meaty version, add 4 oz (125 g) chopped prosciutto cotto or salami.

In a skillet, over medium heat, cook spinach in the water that clings to the leaves, stirring occasionally, for about 8 minutes or until wilted. Drain, let cool slightly and squeeze out excess water. Chop finely and place in a large bowl. Add salt and nutmeg; stir to combine.

In another bowl, whisk together eggs, milk, Grana Padano, basil and pepper; set aside.

Divide tomato, spinach mixture and Asiago among four 1-cup (250 mL) greased ovenproof ramekins or French onion soup bowls. Gently pour in egg mixture. Place bowls on a baking sheet and bake in a 350°F (180°C) oven for about 25 minutes or until a knife inserted in the center comes out clean. (*Let cool, cover and refrigerate for up to 1 day. Serve cold or reheat in microwave.*)

Per serving 250 calories, 20 g protein, 14 g fat, 10 g carbohydrates, 1 g fiber

Eggs in Purgatory Sauce

Uova al Purgatorio

Makes 4 to 6 servings

Eggs in Purgatory has no real religious significance, but since most people who eat Italian food are going to heaven, you don't have to worry anyway, especially when you're enjoying these eggs! This dish is perfect for breakfast, but also makes a quick dinner. Cooking the eggs in tomato sauce gives them added flavor. Serve with crusty Italian bread or buns.

1 tbsp (15 mL) extra-virgin olive oil
2 cloves garlic, minced
1 onion, finely chopped
1 small green bell pepper, diced
¼ tsp (1 mL) hot pepper flakes
1 can (28 oz/796 mL) diced tomatoes
¼ cup (50 mL) chopped fresh Italian parsley
¼ cup (50 mL) chopped fresh basil
¼ tsp (1 mL) salt
8 eggs
¼ cup (50 mL) freshly grated Parmigiano-Reggiano cheese

In a large nonstick skillet, heat oil over medium heat. Add garlic, onion, green pepper and hot pepper flakes; cook, stirring, for 3 minutes or until softened. Add tomatoes, parsley, basil and salt; simmer, uncovered, for 15 minutes or until thickened.

Crack eggs, one at a time, into a small bowl. Gently slide each egg after cracking into tomato sauce. Once all 4 eggs are in, cover and cook for about 4 minutes or until egg whites are set and yolks are to desired doneness. Sprinkle with cheese.

Per each of 6 servings 180 calories, 12 g protein, 10 g fat, 11 g carbohydrates, 3 g fiber

Fried Potatoes, Eggplant and Peppers

Patate, Melanzane e Peperoni Fritti

2 small eggplants, halved lengthwise
  (about 1 lb/500 g total)
⅓ cup (75 mL) extra-virgin olive oil
2 Yukon gold potatoes, peeled and
  thinly sliced (about 8 oz/250 g total)

2 bell peppers, thinly sliced (red,
  yellow or green)
1 clove garlic, minced
½ tsp (2 mL) salt

Slice eggplant halves crosswise into thin slices; set aside.

In a large nonstick skillet, heat ¼ cup (50 mL) of the oil over medium-high heat. Add potatoes and cook, stirring occasionally, for about 8 minutes or until starting to soften. Add eggplant, cover and cook for 5 minutes. Add peppers, garlic and remaining oil; cook, stirring, for about 15 minutes or until golden brown and very tender. Stir in salt.

Makes 4 to 6 servings

I could eat this comfort food by the plateful, on its own or in a bun. If you have leftovers, spread them over a pizza crust and bake in the center of a 425°F (220°C) oven for about 20 minutes or until golden brown; it's tasty hot or cold.

Per each of 6 servings 190 calories, 2 g protein, 13 g fat, 16 g carbohydrates, 4 g fiber

Potato-Stuffed Zucchini

Zucchini Ripieni di Patate

Makes 4 to 6 servings

My grandmother puts this quick dinner together when she's not in the mood for pasta. The moist, creamy combination of potatoes and zucchini is filling and warms you up inside. It's also a delicious side dish for any holiday or family meal.

4 zucchini (about 1 lb/500 g total)
5 Yukon gold potatoes, peeled and
  cubed (about 1½ lbs/750 g total)
2 cloves garlic, minced
¼ cup (50 mL) extra-virgin olive oil
1 egg, lightly beaten
⅓ cup (75 mL) chopped fresh
  Italian parsley

¼ cup (50 mL) freshly grated
  Parmigiano-Reggiano cheese
½ tsp (2 mL) salt
½ tsp (2 mL) freshly ground black
  pepper
Pinch paprika

Trim zucchini and cut in half lengthwise. Using a small spoon, scoop out seeds and some of the flesh, leaving a wall at least ½ inch (1 cm) thick. In a large pot of boiling salted water, cook zucchini for about 8 minutes or until tender-crisp. Remove with a slotted spoon and set aside.

In the same pot of water, cook potatoes for about 20 minutes or until tender. Drain and return to the pot. Using a potato masher, mash potatoes with garlic and 3 tbsp (45 mL) of the oil. Let cool slightly. Stir in egg, parsley, cheese, salt and pepper.

Fill each zucchini half with mashed potato mixture. Place in a single layer in a large shallow greased casserole dish. Sprinkle with paprika and drizzle with the remaining oil. Cover with foil and bake in the center of a 400°F (200°C) oven for about 15 minutes or until steaming and zucchini is tender. Remove foil and bake for 5 minutes or until potatoes are light golden. (*Let cool and place in an airtight container and store in the refrigerator for up to 1 day. Reheat, covered, in 350°F/180°C oven for about 20 minutes or until hot.*)

Per each of 6 servings 240 calories, 6 g protein, 12 g fat, 27 g carbohydrates, 4 g fiber

Cheese-Filled Rice Balls

Arancini

2 cups (500 mL) water
1 tsp (5 mL) saffron threads
1½ cups (375 mL) Arborio rice
½ cup (125 mL) freshly grated
  Romano cheese
2 tbsp (25 mL) butter
3 eggs

6 oz (175 g) mozzarella, provolone,
  Asiago or Havarti cheese
¼ cup (50 mL) all-purpose flour
1 cup (250 mL) seasoned dry
  bread crumbs
6 cups vegetable oil

In a large saucepan, bring water and saffron to a boil. Add rice, reduce heat to low and simmer, stirring frequently, for about 20 minutes or until tender but firm and water is absorbed. Stir in Romano and butter; let cool completely. Stir in 1 of the eggs; set aside.

Meanwhile, cut cheese into 6 cubes; set aside. In a shallow dish, whisk the remaining eggs; set aside.

Form rice mixture into 6 balls. Using your fingers, make an indentation in each ball, fill it with a cheese cube, and seal. Roll balls in flour, then in egg, then in bread crumbs. Place on a baking sheet lined with parchment paper. (*Cover and refrigerate for up to 4 hours.*)

In a large deep saucepan or a deep-fryer, heat oil to 375°F (190°C) over medium heat. Fry balls, in batches, for about 5 minutes or until golden and crispy. Drain on a baking sheet lined with paper towels.

Makes 6 arancini

These gooey rice and cheese bites are delicious warm or cold, alone or with a glass of wine. They make a great snack when you're watching the game. They're called *arancini*, Italian for oranges, because they have the color (from the saffron) and shape of this favorite citrus fruit.

Tips

You can make the balls smaller and serve them as appetizers. Cut cheese into smaller cubes and fry balls for about 2 minutes.

Try other fillings, such as chunks of meat or fish or a chunky meat sauce, and serve with salad.

Per serving 490 calories, 18 g protein, 19 g fat, 61 g carbohydrates, 2 g fiber

Bonnie Stern's Twice-Cooked Minestrone

Ribollita al Forno di Bonnie Stern

Makes 8 to 10 servings

When I first moved to Toronto, I needed a couple of jobs to pay the bills. One was with Bonnie Stern at the Bonnie Stern School of Cooking. What a dream to work with someone whom I had only read about! Bonnie taught me more than she could ever imagine, and she inspired me to teach cooking classes and write recipes. She made it all look so easy. A generous and thoughtful person, Bonnie has remained an inspiration and a great friend. This is her Ribollita recipe from *Simply HeartSmart Cooking.* It's a wonderful vegetarian meal

1 tbsp (15 mL) extra-virgin olive oil
3 cloves garlic, finely chopped
1 onion, chopped
Pinch hot pepper flakes
1 carrot, diced
1 stalk celery, diced
1 zucchini, diced (about 4 oz/125 g)
3 cups (750 mL) chopped cabbage
2 cans (each 28 oz/796 mL) tomatoes
4 cups (1 L) vegetable stock or water
1 can (19 oz/540 mL) white kidney beans, drained and rinsed

1 bunch Swiss chard or rapini, chopped
1 cup (250 mL) pastina
¼ cup (50 mL) chopped fresh basil or Italian parsley
½ tsp (2 mL) freshly ground black pepper
¼ tsp (1 mL) salt
8 thick slices Italian bread
½ cup (125 mL) freshly grated Parmigiano-Reggiano cheese

In a large Dutch oven, heat oil over medium heat. Add garlic, onion and hot pepper flakes; cook, stirring, for about 3 minutes or until softened. Add carrot, celery, zucchini and cabbage; cook, stirring, for about 5 minutes or until cabbage wilts slightly.

Add tomatoes and stock; bring to a boil, breaking up tomatoes with the back of a spoon. Cook for 30 minutes or until vegetables are tender. Add beans, Swiss chard and pastina; cook for 15 minutes. Add basil, black pepper and salt.

Place 4 slices of bread in a 13- x 9-inch (3 L) baking dish, ladle half the soup over top and sprinkle with half the cheese. Repeat layers. Bake in the center of a 350°F (180°C) oven for about 20 minutes or until golden brown and bubbly.

LITTLE PASTA SHAPES

Pastina, the small soup pasta, has endless varieties to choose from. Try tubetti, ditali or stelline for this minestrone. Another small soup pasta favorite is orzo, a rice-shaped pasta perfect for soups and stews.

---

that can be enjoyed with family and friends. The ingredient list may look long, but you're likely to have most of the items in your pantry.

Tips

Serve soup right out of the pot if you don't have time to bake it. Save the leftovers and bake the next night for a thicker, more robust version.

Bonnie's soup calls for cabbage and you can use green or Savoy cabbage. To save a little time, pick up some coleslaw mix in the produce aisle and measure out what you need for the soup. Save the rest to toss into another soup or stew later in the week.

Per each of 10 servings 270 calories, 13 g protein, 4.5 g fat, 44 g carbohydrates, 10 g fiber

risotto and polenta

Rich, creamy and comforting, rice and polenta are two of my favorite things to eat and cook. Growing up with Nana, I got my fair share of polenta, which is a terrific replacement for oatmeal. She would ladle this soft, yellow treat into a bowl, and I would eat it with gusto. I've since learned that it's great cold too, and a delight at any time of day. Try popping it into the microwave for a late-night snack.

Risotto can be prepared in many different ways, whether as a simple rice dish or a flavorful festival of rice, vegetables and seafood. If you have leftovers, try forming risotto into little pancakes and frying them up for breakfast or lunch for a rustic meal that warms the heart and stomach.

Autumn Harvest Risotto

Risotto del Autunno

Makes 4 servings

Daphna Rabinovitch offered me a three-month position as a summer student at *Canadian Living* that flourished into a seven-year job. She is a great friend and mentor who has taught me many things about food and life. She is wise beyond her years, and her passion and flair for cooking is easy to pick up and enjoy— much like her food. Here is her delicious and creamy risotto.

Tip

For the roasted corn kernels, use corn cobs that have been grilled on the barbecue or roasted in the oven. Or, in a skillet, heat 2 tbsp (25 mL) butter or oil and cook canned kernels until golden brown.

¼ cup (50 mL) extra-virgin olive oil
2 shallots, chopped
2 cloves garlic, minced
1 cup (250 mL) sliced shiitake
  mushrooms
½ cup (125 mL) sliced cremini
  mushrooms
½ tsp (2 mL) chopped fresh
  rosemary
½ tsp (2 mL) chopped fresh thyme
Pinch hot pepper flakes
¼ tsp (1 mL) each salt and freshly
  ground black pepper

1 zucchini, diced
1 red bell pepper, diced
1 cup (250 mL) roasted corn
  kernels (see tip, at left)
1½ cups (375 mL) Carnaroli or
  Arborio rice
½ cup (125 mL) dry white wine
4 cups (1 L) hot chicken stock
  (approx) (store-bought or see
  recipe, page 22)
¾ cup (175 mL) freshly grated
  Parmigiano-Reggiano cheese

In a large heavy saucepan, heat half of the oil over medium heat. Add shallots, garlic, shiitake and cremini mushrooms, rosemary, thyme, hot pepper flakes and half each of the salt and black pepper; cook, stirring often, for 3 to 5 minutes or until vegetables are softened. Add zucchini, red pepper and corn; cook for about 5 minutes or until softened and any liquid has evaporated. Scrape into a bowl.

Add remaining oil to pan and stir in rice until well coated. Pour in wine and cook, stirring, until absorbed. Ladle in stock ½ cup (125 mL) at a time, stirring until each addition is absorbed before adding the next, for about 18 minutes or until rice is tender and creamy. Stir in vegetable mixture, ½ cup (125 mL) of the cheese and remaining salt and black pepper. Transfer to a warm serving bowl and sprinkle with remaining cheese.

Per serving 580 calories, 14 g protein, 17 g fat, 88 g carbohydrates, 5 g fiber

Asparagus Risotto

Risotto agli Asparagi

2 tbsp (25 mL) extra-virgin olive oil
2 cloves garlic, minced
1 onion, finely chopped
1½ cups (375 mL) Arborio rice
5 cups (1.25 L) hot chicken or
  vegetable stock (approx) (store-
  bought or see recipe, page 22)

1½ cups (375 mL) chopped
  asparagus
½ cup (125 mL) freshly grated
  Parmigiano-Reggiano cheese
2 tbsp (25 mL) butter
¼ cup (50 mL) chopped fresh basil
  or mint

Makes 4 servings

If you have time, make Parmesan cheese cups to serve this risotto in (see tip, below). Parmesan cups are a classic presentation for some Tuscans. You can also serve them as crisps alongside.

In a large heavy saucepan, heat oil over medium heat. Add garlic and onion; cook, stirring, for about 5 minutes or until softened. Add rice and stir to coat for about 1 minute.

Ladle in stock ½ cup (125 mL) at a time, stirring until each addition is absorbed before adding the next, for about 15 minutes or until rice is al dente (tender but firm to the bite).

Stir in asparagus and cook for about 5 minutes, adding more stock as necessary, until rice is tender and creamy. Remove from heat and stir in cheese and butter until melted and smooth. Sprinkle with basil.

VARIATION
Substitute your favorite vegetable for the asparagus. Try roasted red peppers, chopped cooked carrots, roasted eggplant or peas.

Tip

To make Parmesan cups: For each cup, in a nonstick skillet melt ½ cup (125 mL), freshly grated Parmigiano-Reggiano cheese over medium heat. (Or make 4 small piles of ½ cup (125 mL) each on a baking sheet lined with parchment paper and place in the center of a 400°F / 200°C oven for about 3 minutes or until melted.) Let stand for 30 seconds, then form into bowl shape by draping melted cheese over a small bowl or cup. Let cool until firm.

Per serving 530 calories, 19 g protein, 18 g fat, 74 g carbohydrates, 3 g fiber

Exotic Mushroom Risotto

Risotto ai Funghi

Makes 4 servings

Try a variety of wild mushrooms for a different taste each time you make this dish. This is a recipe my husband, James, has mastered—not bad for a mangia-cake!

Tips

For the exotic mushrooms, try shiitake, oyster, chanterelle, enoki, lobster or morel. If no exotic mushrooms are available, you can use white button or cremini mushrooms; add 3 minutes to the cooking time.

For a deeper mushroom flavor, use dried porcini mushrooms. Soak 1 pkg (3 oz) dried porcini mushrooms in 1 cup (250 mL) boiling water for 15 minutes. Strain through a coffee filter, reserving liquid; rinse mushrooms before cooking. Decrease stock by 1 cup (250 mL) and use soaking liquid.

2 tbsp (25 mL) extra-virgin olive oil	5 cups (1.25 L) hot chicken or vegetable stock (approx) (store-bought or see recipe, page 22)
4 cloves garlic, minced	
1 onion, finely chopped	
1½ cups (375 mL) Arborio rice	½ cup (125 mL) freshly grated Parmigiano-Reggiano cheese
¾ cup (175 mL) dry white wine	
4 cups (1 L) sliced exotic mushrooms (see tip, at left)	2 tbsp (25 mL) butter

In a large heavy saucepan, heat oil over medium heat. Add garlic and onion; cook, stirring, for about 5 minutes or until softened. Add rice and stir to coat for about 1 minute. Add wine and mushrooms; cook, stirring, for about 5 minutes or until wine is absorbed.

Ladle in stock ½ cup (125 mL) at a time, stirring until each addition is absorbed before adding the next, for about 15 minutes or until rice is tender and creamy. Remove from heat and stir in cheese and butter until melted and smooth.

Per serving 580 calories, 20 g protein, 19 g fat, 76 g carbohydrates, 3 g fiber

Seafood Risotto (p. 121)

Chicken Hunter-Style (p. 133)

Chicken Burger (p. 136)

Prosciutto Panini (p. 144)

Roasted Sausages and Peppers (p. 152)

Beef on the Run (p. 158)

Lamb with Artichokes (p. 169)

Pan-fried Tilapia with Caper Wine Sauce (p. 183)

Seafood Risotto

Risotto alla Marinara

2 tbsp (25 mL) extra-virgin olive oil
4 cloves garlic, minced
1 onion, finely chopped
1½ cups (375 mL) Arborio rice
½ cup (125 mL) dry white wine
  (optional)
1½ cups (375 mL) canned or
  fresh diced tomatoes

¼ cup (50 mL) chopped fresh
  oregano
6 cups (1.5 L) hot fish or chicken
  stock (approx) (store-bought or see
  recipe, page 22)
1 lb (500 g) mussels
1 lb (500 g) large raw shrimp, peeled
  and deveined

recipe, page 22

Makes 4 servings

The tomatoes make a rich sauce base for the creamy rice. The shrimp and mussels make this special dish a complete meal.

Tip

For the freshest flavor, buy seafood the same day you want to make the risotto.

In a large shallow Dutch oven, heat oil over medium heat. Add garlic and onion; cook, stirring, for about 5 minutes or until softened. Add rice and stir to coat for about 1 minute. Add wine, if using, and cook, stirring, until evaporated. Add tomatoes and oregano; cook for 5 minutes.

Ladle in stock ½ cup (125 mL) at a time, stirring until each addition is absorbed before adding the next, for about 15 minutes or until rice is al dente (tender but firm to the bite).

Discard any mussels that do not close when tapped. Add mussels and shrimp to rice mixture and stir to combine. Cover and cook for about 10 minutes or until shrimp is pink and opaque, mussels are open and rice is tender and creamy. Discard any mussels that do not open.

Per serving 560 calories, 36 g protein, 12 g fat, 76 g carbohydrates, 3 g fiber

Chicken, Mushroom and Pine Nut Risotto

Risotto con Pollo, Funghi e Pignoli

Makes 4 servings

I met Joanne Leese about seven years ago, and we have remained close friends through the births of her two children and my own—our sons were born only days apart. We are very similar in our approach to motherhood, in our cooking techniques and in that we both love to eat and drink! Our kids have become friends too. Joanne loves to explore flavors with her cooking, and I have had some awesome meals at her home. This is her flavorful and filling risotto.

⅓ cup (75 mL) extra-virgin olive oil
2 boneless skinless chicken breasts, diced (about 8 oz/250 g total)
1 clove garlic, finely chopped
8 oz (250 g) white button mushroom caps, sliced
¼ tsp (1 mL) salt
¼ tsp (1 mL) freshly ground black pepper
¼ cup (50 mL) pine nuts or slivered almonds
1½ cups (375 mL) Arborio rice
5 cups (1.25 L) hot chicken stock (store-bought or see recipe, page 22)
½ cup (125 mL) freshly grated Parmigiano-Reggiano cheese
1 tbsp (15 mL) chopped fresh Italian parsley

In a large heavy saucepan, heat 2 tbsp (25 mL) of the oil over medium heat. Add chicken and garlic; cook, stirring, for 5 minutes. Add mushrooms, salt and pepper; cook, stirring occasionally, for about 5 minutes or until mushrooms soften and chicken is no longer pink inside. Scrape into a bowl.

Meanwhile, in a small skillet, heat 1 tbsp (15 mL) of the oil over medium heat. Add pine nuts and cook for about 3 minutes or until golden brown; set aside.

In the same heavy saucepan, heat the remaining oil over medium heat. Add rice and stir to coat for about 1 minute. Ladle in stock ½ cup (125 mL) at a time, stirring until each addition is absorbed before adding the next, for about 15 minutes or until rice is al dente (tender but firm to the bite). Add any remaining stock, chicken mixture, cheese and parsley; stir to combine until creamy. Transfer to a warm serving bowl and sprinkle with pine nuts.

Per serving 690 calories, 34 g protein, 29 g fat, 73 g carbohydrates, 2 g fiber

Rice Soup

Zuppa di Riso

2 tbsp (25 mL) extra-virgin olive oil
2 cloves garlic, minced
1 small onion, chopped
1 carrot, finely chopped
1 stalk celery, finely chopped
¼ tsp (1 mL) hot pepper flakes
1 cup (250 mL) Arborio rice
2 Yukon gold potatoes, peeled and
  diced (about 6 oz/175 g total)
1 tomato, chopped (optional)

1 bay leaf
6 cups (1.5 L) vegetable or chicken
  stock (store-bought or see recipe,
  page 22)
¼ cup (50 mL) chopped fresh Italian
  parsley
Pinch salt
Pinch freshly ground black pepper
3 tbsp (45 mL) freshly grated
  Romano cheese

Makes 4 servings

This is kind of like a risotto but a bit soupier. It's an adaptation of what my grandmother and mother make, and is a little quicker to put together than a traditional risotto. When you are feeling under the weather, this "carb-packed" dinner really hits the spot.

In a large deep heavy saucepan, heat oil over medium heat. Add garlic, onion, carrot, celery and hot pepper flakes; cook, stirring, for about 5 minutes or until softened. Add rice and stir to coat for about 1 minute. Add potatoes, tomato (if using), bay leaf, stock and parsley; bring to a boil. Reduce heat and simmer, uncovered, for about 15 minutes or until rice and potato are tender. Remove bay leaf and stir in salt and black pepper. Ladle into bowls and sprinkle with cheese.

VARIATION
If you have some chopped or sliced cabbage in the fridge, add it with the potatoes. It adds another dimension of flavor and texture. All you need is about 2 cups (500 mL).

Per serving 420 calories, 15 g protein, 11 g fat, 65 g carbohydrates, 3 g fiber

Sausage and Tomato Polenta

Polenta di Salsiccia e Pomodoro

Makes 8 servings

I could eat this for breakfast, I love it so much. My grand-mother still makes it best, I admit, but this is pretty close to hers. We call this "farinata" at our house because the cornmeal is so smooth, much like farina.

1 tbsp (15 mL) extra-virgin olive oil
4 mild Italian sausages, casings
  removed
½ tsp (2 mL) hot pepper flakes
1 can (28 oz/796 mL) crushed
  tomatoes
13 cups (3.25 L) water (approx)
4½ tsp (22 mL) salt
1 tbsp (15 mL) dried oregano

Polenta
2 cups (500 mL) cornmeal
½ cup (125 mL) freshly grated
  Parmigiano-Reggiano or Romano
  cheese
½ cup (125 mL) chopped fresh
  Italian parsley

In a large nonstick skillet, heat oil over medium-high heat. Add sausages and hot pepper flakes; cook, breaking up sausages with the back of a spoon, for about 8 minutes or until no longer pink inside. Add tomatoes, 1 cup (250 mL) of the water, ½ tsp (2 mL) of the salt and oregano; bring to a boil. Reduce heat and simmer, uncovered, for about 25 minutes or until thickened.

Polenta: Meanwhile, in a large heavy saucepan or Dutch oven, bring 10 cups (2.5 L) of the water and 4 tsp (20 mL) of the salt to a boil. Slowly whisk in corn-meal until thickened. Reduce heat to low and simmer, stirring often with a wooden spoon, for about 20 minutes or until smooth and very creamy, adding water as necessary to maintain creaminess.

Add half of the sausage mixture to the saucepan and stir to combine. Cook, stirring, for about 10 minutes to allow flavors to blend. Stir in half each of the cheese and parsley. Transfer to a warm serving bowl, top with the remaining sausage mixture and sprinkle with the remaining cheese and parsley.

ITALIAN SAUSAGE

Aside from the heat level, there is not much difference between mild and hot Italian sausages. Pork sausages are the most common, but you can find pork and veal combinations as well. The hot ones have hot pepper flakes and sometimes hot pepper sauce added. Sausages vary a lot, depending on who makes them and where you buy them. Try a few different kinds to see which you prefer. If you like the taste of fennel, look for sausages that include it.

Tip

If you want to make the polenta mixture quickly, use a quick-cooking polenta, which is simply a finer cornmeal that absorbs water and thickens more quickly. You'll find it in Italian delis and some grocery stores.

Per serving 290 calories, 13 g protein, 13 g fat, 31 g carbohydrates, 4 g fiber

Polenta with Red Pepper and Sausage Sauce

Polenta con Ragu di Peperoni e Salsiccia

Makes 4 servings

One of Elizabeth Baird's favorite meals to serve her family is sausage, and she makes it more homey and Italian by stirring up some polenta to go with it. I grew up eating polenta, and it really does fill you up, especially on cold winter nights.

3 lean mild or hot Italian sausages (about 12 oz/375 g total)
1 tbsp (15 mL) extra-virgin olive oil
4 cloves garlic, minced
2 large onions, chopped
2 bay leaves
1 red bell pepper, diced
1 tsp (5 mL) crumbled dried oregano
½ tsp (2 mL) fennel seeds, crushed (see tip, page 127)
Pinch hot pepper flakes
1 can (28 oz/796 mL) diced tomatoes
1 cup (250 mL) vegetable or chicken stock (store-bought or see recipe, page 22)
2 tbsp (25 mL) tomato paste

Polenta
4 cups (1 L) water
½ tsp (2 mL) salt
1 cup (250 mL) cornmeal
¼ cup (50 mL) minced fresh Italian parsley
¼ cup (50 mL) freshly grated Parmigiano-Reggiano, Romano or Grana Padano cheese

Cut sausages into chunks. In large heavy saucepan or Dutch oven, heat oil over medium-high heat. Add sausage and brown on all sides. Using a slotted spoon, transfer sausage to a plate; set aside.

Reduce heat to medium-low and add garlic, onions, bay leaves, red pepper, oregano, fennel and hot pepper flakes; cook, stirring occasionally, for about 8 minutes or until vegetables are softened. Add browned sausage, tomatoes, stock and tomato paste; increase heat and bring to a boil. Reduce heat and simmer, stirring often, for about 30 minutes or until thickened. Remove bay leaves.

Polenta: Meanwhile, in a medium saucepan, bring water and salt to a boil. In a thin, steady stream, whisk in cornmeal; bring back to a boil. Reduce heat and simmer, stirring almost constantly, for about 15 minutes or until polenta mounds firmly on a spoon. Stir in parsley and cheese.

Spoon polenta into warmed pasta bowls and top with a generous ladleful of sauce.

MORE POLENTA IDEAS

Other things to add to polenta: cook some mushrooms and garlic and stir them in or serve on top with a sprinkling of Asiago cheese. You can also serve the polenta with the Bolognese sauce from page 163.

Try adding other vegetables such as corn kernels, red pepper or shredded spinach into the polenta while cooking.

Let the polenta firm up by pouring it into a 13 X 9 inch (3 L) baking dish and refrigerating overnight. Cut into small pieces and grill or fry in skillet and serve with pasta sauce or grilled or roasted vegetables.

Tip

Fennel seeds add an elusive licorice flavor to this robust sauce. Crush them lightly using a mortar and pestle, or enclose them in a bag and crush on a board with the bottom of a heavy pot.

Per serving 460 calories, 21 g protein, 19 g fat, 52 g carbohydrates, 9 g fiber

chicken and game

In many homes, chicken is the most popular protein choice. It's certainly a hit at my house. One of the reasons is that chicken can adapt to any flavor; it's perfect with pesto and succulent with sauce. And when grilled to perfection, like Chicken under Bricks (page 134), it's sure to impress your guests.

In everything from sandwiches to skillet dinners, chicken is a versatile and delicious ingredient. Whether your family prefers drumsticks, breasts or thighs, you will find a dish they'll enjoy among the recipes in this chapter. Don't forget to save the bones—they're great for making stock.

Chicken Cutlets with Cheese

Fettine di Pollo con Formaggio

Makes 6 servings

This has been one of my all-time favorites since I was a kid. And all the children in my extended family love it—some dishes are classics. These cutlets freeze well after frying. Heat them up to enjoy for another dinner or in a sandwich. I've been known to eat them cold for breakfast!

6 boneless skinless chicken breasts
 (about 1½ lbs/ 750 g total)
3 eggs
¼ tsp (1 mL) salt
2 cups (500 mL) dry bread crumbs
2 tbsp (25 mL) freshly grated
 Parmigiano-Reggiano cheese

½ cup (125 mL) canola or vegetable
 oil (approx)
6 slices provolone cheese
2 tbsp (25 mL) chopped fresh
 Italian parsley

Remove tenders from chicken breasts and set aside. Place 2 chicken breasts at a time between 2 large pieces of parchment paper. Using a meat mallet, pound breasts out to about ½ inch (1 cm) thick. Repeat with remaining breasts.

In a shallow dish, whisk together eggs and salt. Add chicken breasts and tenders; turn to coat. In another shallow dish, combine bread crumbs and Parmigiano-Reggiano. Remove one chicken breast from egg mixture and let excess drip off. Add to bread crumb mixture and turn to coat evenly. Place on a baking sheet lined with waxed paper. Repeat with remaining chicken breasts and tenders.

In a large nonstick skillet, heat half of the oil over medium-high heat. Add chicken, in batches, and cook, turning once, for about 6 minutes or until golden brown on both sides and no longer pink inside. Remove to a plate lined with paper towels. Repeat with remaining chicken, adding oil as necessary. *(Let cool completely. Place between waxed paper in airtight container and freeze for up to 1 month.)* Top each breast with a slice of provolone and place in a 375°F (190°C) oven for about 5 minutes or until cheese melts. Sprinkle with parsley.

VARIATIONS

For a saucy version, top chicken with a little pasta sauce before adding cheese.

Try other cheeses, such as Asiago, smoked provolone or mozzarella. In Italy, they would use Fette di Fondi cheese slices, a processed cheese used in sauces and on sandwiches. Our version—white cheese slices—would work too.

Per serving 410 calories, 36 g protein, 22 g fat, 18 g carbohydrates, 1 g fiber

Balsamic Chicken and Mushrooms

Pollo e Funghi all'Aceto Balsamico

Makes 4 servings

The sweet balsamic vinegar is absorbed by the mushrooms and glazes the chicken while it roasts. This dish is quick enough for a weeknight meal; simply place it in the oven while you prepare a green salad and mashed potatoes.

Tip

You can use all button or cremini mushrooms or substitute oyster mushrooms for the shiitake mushrooms.

4 skinless bone-in chicken breasts (about 2 lbs/1 kg total)
4 tsp (20 mL) chopped fresh thyme
½ tsp (2 mL) salt
½ tsp (2 mL) freshly ground black pepper
1 tbsp (15 mL) extra-virgin olive oil
6 cloves garlic, minced

8 oz (250 g) button or cremini mushrooms, sliced
8 oz (250 g) shiitake mushrooms, stemmed and sliced
1 cup (250 mL) grape tomatoes
⅓ cup (75 mL) balsamic vinegar
3 tbsp (45 mL) chopped fresh basil

Sprinkle chicken evenly with half each of the thyme, salt and pepper. In a large nonstick skillet, heat oil over medium-high heat. Add chicken breasts and brown on both sides. Using tongs, remove chicken to a large casserole dish.

To the oil remaining in the skillet, add garlic, button and shiitake mushrooms and the remaining thyme, salt and pepper; cook, stirring, for about 8 minutes or until vegetables are softened and beginning to turn golden. Remove from heat and stir in tomatoes and vinegar.

Pour vegetable mixture over chicken and roast in a 400°F (200°C) oven for about 20 minutes or until chicken is no longer pink inside and reaches an internal temperature of 170°F (75°C). Sprinkle with basil.

Per serving 230 calories, 30 g protein, 7 g fat, 11 g carbohydrates, 2 g fiber

Chicken Hunter-Style

Pollo Cacciatore

1 lb (500 g) chicken drumsticks
1 lb (500 g) chicken thighs
¼ tsp (1 mL) salt
¼ tsp (1 mL) freshly ground black
  pepper
2 tbsp (25 mL) extra-virgin olive oil
4 cloves garlic, minced
1 onion, chopped

1 red bell pepper, chopped
1 green bell pepper, chopped
1 lb (500 g) mushrooms, quartered
1 tbsp (15 mL) dried oregano
1 tsp (5 mL) dried basil
½ cup (125 mL) dry white wine
1 can (28 oz/796 mL) diced tomatoes

Makes 6 servings

Cacciatore means "hunter," and chicken cacciatore offers up chunks of vegetables and chicken in a rich tomato-vegetable sauce that Italian hunters would enjoy during their expeditions. I serve this dish with tagliatelle or fettuccine to soak up the sauce.

Tip
Use all drumsticks or all thighs, if desired.

Sprinkle chicken drumsticks and thighs evenly with salt and pepper. In a large shallow Dutch oven, heat half of the oil over medium-high heat. Add chicken and brown on both sides. Using tongs, remove chicken to a plate.

In same pot, heat the remaining oil over medium-high heat. Add garlic, onion, red and green peppers, mushrooms, oregano and basil; cook over medium-high heat, stirring, for about 15 minutes or until vegetables are beginning to brown. Pour in wine, stirring and scraping up any brown bits from bottom of pot. Add tomatoes and bring to a boil. Return chicken to pot. Reduce heat, cover and simmer for about 20 minutes or until juices run clear when chicken is pierced. *(Let cool. Cover and refrigerate for up to 2 days. Reheat on medium-low heat until heated through.)*

VARIATION
Rabbit Hunter-Style: Substitute 2 lbs (1 kg) rabbit pieces for the chicken and add 20 minutes to cooking time. Some grocery stores sell whole rabbits, but butchers will cut the rabbit into smaller pieces for you.

Per serving 290 calories, 23 g protein, 15 g fat, 15 g carbohydrates, 4 g fiber

Chicken under Bricks

Pollo al Mattone

Makes 4 servings

Traditionally, "chicken under bricks" was cooked in a brick oven and flattened with more bricks. This process helps decrease the cooking time while intensifying the flavor. You will need 2 standard house bricks for this recipe. Wrap them well with foil.

Tips

Experiment with your own combination of fresh herbs—try thyme, basil and oregano. Or use a dried herb combination, such as my Italian Herb Seasoning Mix (see recipe, page 17). You will need 1 heaping tbsp (15 mL).

You could have your butcher butterfly the chicken for you.

Be sure to turn the bricks over when you turn the chicken as well.

1 whole chicken (about 3 lbs/1.5 kg)
2 tbsp (25 mL) extra-virgin olive oil
2 tbsp (25 mL) chopped fresh sage
2 tbsp (25 mL) chopped fresh rosemary
½ tsp (2 mL) salt
½ tsp (2 mL) freshly ground black pepper

Using kitchen shears or strong scissors, cut chicken along each side of the backbone; remove backbone. Turn chicken over and push on the breastbone to make chicken lie flat. Tuck wings behind back, or trim if desired. Place chicken in a large shallow baking dish. Brush with half of the oil and sprinkle evenly with sage, rosemary, salt and pepper.

In a large nonstick skillet, heat the remaining oil over medium heat (or heat grill to medium-high). Add chicken skin side down and place bricks on top. Cook for 20 minutes. Remove bricks and turn chicken. Replace bricks and cook for about 15 minutes longer or until juices run clear when a leg is pierced. Cut into serving-size pieces.

Per serving 450 calories, 48 g protein, 27 g fat, 1 g carbohydrates, 0 g fiber

Breaded "Italian Style" Chicken Wings

Pollo Cotto al Forno

2 lbs (1 kg) chicken drumettes
2 tbsp (25 mL) extra-virgin olive oil
1 cup (250 mL) seasoned dry bread
  crumbs
¼ cup (50 mL) freshly grated
  Parmigiano-Reggiano cheese

1 tsp (5 mL) Italian herb seasoning
  (store-bought or see recipe, page 17)
¼ tsp (1 mL) hot pepper flakes
¼ tsp (1 mL) salt
¼ tsp (1 mL) freshly ground black
  pepper

In a large bowl, toss chicken with oil to coat evenly.

In a small bowl, combine bread crumbs, cheese, Italian herb seasoning, hot pepper flakes, salt and black pepper. Sprinkle over chicken and toss to coat well.

Spread chicken drumettes in a single layer on a baking sheet lined with parchment paper. Bake in the bottom third of a 400°F (200°C) oven, turning once, for about 30 minutes or until juices run clear when chicken is pierced.

Makes 4 servings

I know chicken wings are not very Italian, but these drumettes, with their blend of traditional Italian seasonings, might just change that trend. My son and husband enjoy these on weeknights when we want to watch a show and take it easy—I wish that was every night!

Tips

Chicken drumettes are the parts of chicken wings that resemble small drumsticks.

Dip drumettes in hot pasta or pizza sauce for a great chicken parmigiana taste.

Per serving 450 calories, 30 g protein, 27 g fat, 22 g carbohydrates, 1 g fiber

Chicken Burgers

Hamburger di Pollo

Makes 4 servings

When we think burgers, we think buns. Italians, however, serve the meat with the bread on the side. But they have mastered cooking terrific patties, which they make from beef, veal, pork, sausage and, as here, chicken.

Tip

If you want, you can put the patty on the bread and top it with the tomato for an open-faced sandwich. Of course, these burgers are also delicious in regular hamburger buns.

1 lb (500 g) ground chicken
3 tbsp (45 mL) extra-virgin olive oil
1 tsp (5 mL) finely chopped fresh rosemary
½ tsp (2 mL) salt
½ tsp (2 mL) freshly ground black pepper
4 slices thick crusty bread
1 tomato, sliced

In a medium bowl, combine chicken, 2 tbsp (25 mL) of the oil, rosemary, salt and pepper. Form into four ¼-inch (5 mm) patties. *(Cover and refrigerate for up to 8 hours.)*

In a large nonstick skillet, heat the remaining oil over medium-high heat. Cook patties, in batches if necessary, turning once, for about 8 minutes or until they are no longer pink inside.

Serve with bread and tomatoes.

Per serving 330 calories, 22 g protein, 21 g fat, 12 g carbohydrates, 1 g fiber

Pesto Chicken and Asiago Baguette

Panini di Pollo con Pesto ed Asiago

4 boneless skinless chicken breasts (about 1 lb/500 g total)
1 tbsp (15 mL) extra-virgin olive oil
½ tsp (2 mL) dried oregano
Pinch salt
Pinch freshly ground black pepper
1 cup (250 mL) pesto (store-bought or see recipe, page 18)
2 French baguettes or Vienna loaves

1 cup (250 mL) Roasted Garlic Aioli (see recipe, page 19)
2 cups (500 mL) lightly packed fresh baby spinach
1½ cups (375 mL) shaved Asiago cheese
½ cup (125 mL) slivered oil-packed sun-dried tomatoes, drained

The combination of chicken and pesto makes for a perfect summer sandwich, and the spicy Asiago adds just the right zing!

Slice chicken breasts in half horizontally. In a bowl, combine oil, oregano, salt and pepper. Add chicken and turn to coat evenly. Place on a greased grill over medium-high heat and brush with some of the pesto. Cook, turning once, for about 5 minutes or until chicken is no longer pink inside. Let cool.

Cut baguettes in half; then cut each half again horizontally. Spread cut sides with aioli. Place chicken on bottom halves and spread with remaining pesto. Top with spinach, cheese and sun-dried tomatoes. Cover with top halves of baguettes. *(Wrap in plastic wrap and refrigerate for up to 8 hours.)*

Per each of 6 servings 590 calories, 35 g protein, 18 g fat, 73 g carbohydrates, 6 g fiber

Chicken and Roasted Red Pepper Sandwich

Panini con Pollo e Peperoni Rostiti

Makes 2 servings

Roasted peppers, fo-
caccia, pesto, olives . . .
what could be more
Italian? Feel free to
use different cheeses,
meats and greens to
suit your mood or
taste—there are
countless possible
combinations!

8 oz (250 g) boneless skinless
  chicken breasts
1 tbsp (15 mL) Dijon mustard
Pinch salt
Pinch freshly ground black pepper
1 loaf rosemary focaccia
¼ cup (50 mL) mayonnaise

2 tbsp (25 mL) pesto (store-bought
  or see recipe, page 18)
1 cup (250 mL) trimmed arugula
2 roasted red bell peppers, thinly
  sliced
⅓ cup (75 mL) shaved Parmigiano-
  Reggiano cheese

Brush chicken breasts with mustard and sprinkle evenly with salt and pepper. In a grill pan or nonstick skillet, cook chicken, turning once, for about 10
minutes or until it is no longer pink inside. Let cool completely, then slice on
the diagonal into thin slices.

Slice focaccia in half horizontally. In a small bowl, combine mayonnaise and
pesto. Spread over focaccia bottom and top with chicken and arugula, alter-
nating colors. Top with roasted red peppers and cheese. Cover with top half
of focaccia and cut in half. *(Cover and refrigerate for up to 4 hours.)*

Per serving 1010 calories, 49 g protein, 47 g fat, 97 g carbohydrates, 6 g fiber

Tomato Braised Rabbit

Coniglio in Umido al Pomodoro

1 rabbit, cleaned and cut into pieces
  (about 2½ lbs/1.25 kg)
½ tsp (2 mL) salt
½ tsp (2 mL) freshly ground black
  pepper
2 tbsp (25 mL) extra-virgin olive oil
4 cloves garlic, chopped
1 large onion, finely diced
1 large carrot, finely diced
1 stalk celery, finely diced
1½ cups (375 mL) dry white wine

¼ cup (50 mL) tomato paste
1 can (28 oz/796 mL) diced tomatoes
1 bay leaf
½ cup (125 mL) chopped fresh
  Italian parsley
½ cup (125 mL) chopped fresh basil
¼ cup (50 mL) dried porcini
  mushrooms
2 tbsp (25 mL) chopped fresh sage
1 tbsp (15 mL) chopped fresh
  rosemary

Makes 6 to 8 servings

I met chef Roberto Fracchioni a couple of years ago. He was the executive chef at Inn on the Twenty in Niagara for a number of years, and is a fellow Italian and friend. I have tasted his food many times and have always enjoyed it. He is influenced by his heritage and his years of experience cooking in Italy. His rabbit dish takes a bit of time, but is well worth it. Rabbit is eaten frequently throughout Italy and has always been a favorite of mine, but you can use chicken if you prefer.

Sprinkle rabbit with salt and pepper. In a large Dutch oven, heat oil over medium-high heat. Add rabbit and brown on all sides. Using tongs, remove rabbit to a plate.

To the oil remaining in the pot, add garlic, onion, carrot and celery; reduce heat to medium and cook, stirring, for about 5 minutes or until softened. Add wine and tomato paste; bring to a boil. Boil for 3 minutes or until reduced slightly. Add tomatoes, bay leaf, parsley, basil, mushrooms, sage and rosemary; return to a boil. Return rabbit to pot; cover and simmer, stirring occasionally, for about 40 minutes or until rabbit is tender. (*Let cool. Cover and refrigerate for up to 1 day. Reheat over medium-low until heated through.*)

Per each of 8 servings 250 calories, 27 g protein, 10 g fat, 13 g carbohydrates, 4 g fiber

Roasted Quail with Fennel

Quaglia Arrostita con Finocchio

Makes 3 to 4 servings

My sister, Tina Fernandes, loves to cook. One of her favorites is quail, and she whipped this dish up for us one night. It was so good it had to go into the book. You'll have to eat with your hands to enjoy every bit of the flavorful meat.

Tip
Look for quail at your local butcher or in the freezer section of the grocery store.

6 quail (about 1¼ lbs/625 g total)
¾ tsp (4 mL) salt
¾ tsp (4 mL) freshly ground black pepper
3 tbsp (45 mL) extra-virgin olive oil
2 cloves garlic, minced

1 bulb fennel, cut in large chunks
1 large carrot, sliced
½ cup (125 mL) chopped onion
½ cup (125 mL) balsamic vinegar
2 tbsp (25 mL) chopped fresh Italian parsley

Using kitchen shears or strong scissors, cut quail along the backbone; press gently on the breastbone to make quail lie flat. Sprinkle with ½ tsp (2 mL) each of the salt and pepper. In a large nonstick skillet, heat 1 tbsp (15 mL) of the oil over medium-high heat. Add quail, in batches, and brown well, turning once.

Meanwhile, in a 13- x 9-inch (3 L) baking dish, toss together the remaining oil, garlic, fennel, carrot and onion. Sprinkle with the remaining salt and pepper and toss to combine. Place quail on top of vegetables. Roast in the top third of a 425°F (220°C) oven for 20 minutes or until fennel is tender and quail has only a hint of pink inside. Drizzle vinegar over quail and cook for 5 minutes or until glazed.

Mound vegetables on a serving dish and top with quail. Drizzle with pan juices and sprinkle with parsley.

Per each of 4 servings 460 calories, 34 g protein, 30 g fat, 14 g carbohydrates, 3 g fiber

Hearty Penne Pasta

Penne Abbondante

1 tbsp (15 mL) extra-virgin olive oil
4 oz (125 g) ground venison or veal
4 cups (1 L) packed thinly sliced
  Swiss chard leaves
4 cloves garlic, minced
½ tsp (2 mL) hot pepper flakes

1 cup (250 mL) canned tomatoes
  with their juices
1 cup (250 mL) chicken stock
Pinch each salt and pepper
4 cups (1 L) penne rigate
¼ cup (50 mL) freshly grated
  Parmigiano-Reggiano cheese

In Northern Ontario where I was born, game meats are very popular. I remember having moose meat in the freezer and trying to figure out how were we going to make that Italian! Well, here is your opportunity to make a quick sauce with venison, moose or ground chicken, whatever you have in the freezer. Just be sure to thaw it first!

In large saucepan, heat oil over medium-high heat and cook venison for about 5 minutes or until no longer pink. Add Swiss chard and cook, stirring, for about 4 minutes or until wilted. Add garlic and chili flakes and cook, stirring, for 1 minute. Add tomatoes, stock, salt and pepper and bring to boil. Reduce heat and simmer for about 15 minutes or until thickened with some juices remaining.

Meanwhile, in large pot of boiling salted water cook pasta for about 10 minutes or until al dente (tender but firm to the the bite). Drain well and return to pot. Add Swiss chard sauce and toss with pasta to coat. Add cheese and toss to combine.

Vegetarian Option: Omit venison and add 1 can (19 oz) white kidney beans, drained and rinsed with tomatoes.

Per serving 460 calories, 23 g protein, 8 g fat, 74 g carbohydrates, 4 g fiber

pork and sausage

Pork is versatile and is used widely in Italy for roasts and with many different sauces. One of my favorite food memories is seeing a roast pig on a spit for the first time and tasting the crispy, crunchy skin and fall-apart-tender meat. It was far beyond anything I had tasted before. No one has time during the week to prepare a roast pig, but the quick cuts of pork available in markets make it easy to enjoy.

I love making sausages with my dad; frankly, he makes them best. He has taught me to appreciate the time that goes into a truly unique and delicious product. The quality of homemade sausage simply cannot be beat. As I grill up freshly made sausages, I anticipate the moment I'll bite into the crisp casing and feel the juices spatter my face. It's at moments like these that I realize how much I love what I do. I'm so privileged to be able to share these experiences with you.

Prosciutto Panini

Panini al Prosciutto

Makes 4 servings

Sandwiches are quick and easy and are wonderful for dinner. They can be filled with endless varieties of meat, cheese or vegetables. Here is a sandwich my family enjoys frequently. Great for dinners on the run!

Tips

Bocconcini are fresh mozzarella balls that are packed in water so they'll stay fresh. Look for them in bulk in the deli or in plastic tubs in the cheese aisle. You can buy 4 large bocconcini or 8 smaller ones for this sandwich. Mini or cherry-size bocconcini make delicious snacks or hors d'oeuvres.

In and around Rome, panini are usually heated through in a panini press or sandwich grill.

4 ciabatta buns, halved horizontally
1 tbsp (15 mL) extra-virgin olive oil
12 thin slices prosciutto

1 cup (250 mL) trimmed arugula
  leaves
4 bocconcini, thinly sliced
Balsamic vinegar (optional)

Drizzle bottom halves of buns with oil. Top with prosciutto, arugula leaves and bocconcini. Drizzle with balsamic vinegar, if desired. Cover with top halves of buns.

GRILLING PANINI

To grill panini, use a press or place your sandwich on a grill or grill pan and weight it down to heat the sandwich and melt the cheese slightly. Turn and do the same on the other side until the crust is golden brown.

Per serving 380 calories, 19 g protein, 19 g fat, 33 g carbohydrates, 2 g fiber

Italian Express

Pork Chops

Braciole di Maiale

4 lean bone-in pork loin chops
 (about 1½ lbs/750 kg total)
¼ tsp (1 mL) salt

¼ tsp (1 mL) freshly ground black
 pepper
¼ cup (50 mL) extra-virgin olive oil
4 lemon wedges

Makes 4 servings

I enjoyed this simple pork dish for lunch in Rome with a salad and a beer (which cost the same as a soft drink!). Dressed lightly with oil and a squeeze of lemon, this makes a quick dinner for the family. Use a good-quality extra-virgin olive oil with a fruity olive flavor to enhance the pork.

Trim any excess fat from pork and sprinkle evenly with salt and pepper. In a large nonstick skillet, heat half of the oil over medium-high heat. Add pork and brown on both sides. Reduce heat to medium, cover and cook for about 8 minutes or until juices run clear when pork is pierced and just a hint of pink remains inside.

Transfer pork to plates, drizzle with the remaining oil and squeeze with lemon.

VARIATION
Substitute veal chops for the pork chops.

Per serving 220 calories, 19 g protein, 15 g fat, 1 g carbohydrates, 0 g fiber

Garlic Rosemary Pork Chops with Tomato Pesto Drizzle

Braciole di Maiale con Aglio, Rosmarino e Pomodoro con Pesto

Makes 6 servings

Garlic and rosemary are a perfect match with pork, and garlic has a natural link with pesto. You can grill these chops in summer or pan-fry year-round. Serve with grilled or roasted vegetables, or green beans tossed with a red wine vinaigrette.

Tips

If you like, buy your own pork loin and cut chops to the perfect thickness. I like mine about ¾ inch (2 cm) thick.

If you prefer to pan-fry rather than grill, heat a nonstick skillet over medium-high heat, and cook pork, turning once, for about 15 minutes or until juices run clear when pork is pierced and just a hint of pink remains inside.

8 cloves garlic, minced
¼ cup (50 mL) extra-virgin olive oil
4 tsp (20 mL) chopped fresh rosemary
2 tsp (10 mL) chopped fresh thyme
¼ tsp (1 mL) hot pepper flakes
Pinch salt
Pinch freshly ground black pepper
6 boneless thick-cut butterfly pork loin chops (about 2 lbs/1 kg total)
12 slices prosciutto

Tomato Pesto Drizzle
¼ cup (50 mL) extra-virgin olive oil
2 tbsp (25 mL) pesto (store-bought or see recipe, page 18)
2 tbsp (25 mL) red wine vinegar
Pinch salt
1½ cups (375 mL) grape tomatoes, halved

In a shallow dish, stir together garlic, oil, rosemary, thyme, hot pepper flakes, salt and black pepper. Add pork and turn to coat evenly. Wrap each chop with 2 slices of prosciutto.

Place pork on a greased grill, over medium-high heat, and grill, turning once, for about 12 minutes or until juices run clear when pork is pierced and just a hint of pink remains inside.

Tomato Pesto Drizzle: Meanwhile, in a small bowl, whisk together oil, pesto, vinegar and salt. Add tomatoes and toss to coat. Serve as a sauce with pork chops.

Per serving 480 calories, 35 g protein, 36 g fat, 4 g carbohydrates, 1 g fiber

Stuffed Pork Rolls

Braciole di Maiale Ripiene

1 boneless center-cut single loin
  pork roast (about 2 lbs/1 kg)
1 small head garlic, peeled and
  minced
1 cup (250 mL) chopped fresh
  Italian parsley

½ tsp (2 mL) salt
½ tsp (2 mL) freshly ground black
  pepper
¼ cup (50 mL) extra-virgin olive oil
4 cups (1 L) pasta sauce (store-
  bought or see recipe, page 20)

Makes 6 to 8 servings

My mother and my
dad's oldest sister,
Zia Peppina, who also
calls these "vra sciole"
in Calabrese dialect,
love these rolls. By
cutting the meat your-
self, you control the
thickness. For quicker
braciole, purchase
pork or veal cutlets al-
ready cut at your meat
counter. They may
need some pounding
to thin them out a bit.

Tips

**Be sure to tell your guests
about the toothpicks!**

**Serve the extra sauce tossed
with your favorite pasta or
gnocchi.**

Thinly slice pork lengthwise into cutlets; lay out flat. Using a meat pounder, flatten pork if uneven. Spread cutlets with garlic, parsley and salt and pepper. Roll up crosswise and secure with kitchen string or a toothpick.

In a large saucepan, heat oil over medium-high heat. Add braciole and brown on all sides. Reduce heat to medium, cover and cook for about 10 minutes or until juices run clear when pork is pierced and just a hint of pink remains inside. Add pasta sauce, cover and simmer for about 20 minutes or until pork is very tender. *(Let cool. Cover and refrigerate for up to 2 days. Reheat over medium-low heat until heated through.)*

VARIATION
Sprinkle cheese on the cutlets before rolling them up. Use about ½ cup (125 mL) freshly grated Parmigiano-Reggiano, shredded Asiago or shredded provolone piccante.

Per each of 8 servings including ⅛th of sauce 290 calories, 23 g protein, 16 g fat, 14 g carbohydrates, 3 g fiber

Pork Stew

Ragu di Carne di Maiale

Makes 4 servings

Pork is an important meat to the Italians; they use the pig for everything it has. This stew showcases a lean cut of loin and pancetta (pork belly that has been rolled and salt-cured). Serve with potatoes or simply prepared vegetables, such as steamed green beans. This stew is also delicious made with veal.

Tip

Toss your favorite pasta with this stew for a hearty pasta dish.

2 tbsp (25 mL) extra-virgin olive oil	1 lb (500 g) lean pork loin, cut into
6 slices pancetta, chopped	½-inch (1 cm) cubes
1 small onion, chopped	1 can (5½ oz/156 mL) tomato paste
1 carrot, chopped	1 bay leaf
1 stalk celery, chopped	2 cups (500 mL) beef stock
½ tsp (2 mL) dried basil	½ tsp (2 mL) salt
½ tsp (2 mL) dried oregano	Pinch freshly ground black pepper
Pinch hot pepper flakes	

In a large saucepan, heat oil over medium-high heat. Add pancetta, onion, carrot, celery, basil, oregano and hot pepper flakes; cook, stirring, for 5 minutes or until softened. Add pork and cook, stirring, for 2 minutes. Add tomato paste, bay leaf and stock; bring to a boil. Reduce heat, cover and simmer for about 15 minutes or until juices run clear when pork is pierced and just a hint of pink remains inside. Remove bay leaf and add salt and black pepper. *(Let cool. Cover and refrigerate for up to 2 days. Reheat over medium-low heat until heated through.)*

Per serving 390 calories, 33 g protein, 22 g fat, 16 g carbohydrates, 4 g fiber

Stuffed Portobello Mushrooms

Funghi Ripieni

1 tbsp (15 mL) extra-virgin olive oil
4 cloves garlic, minced
1 onion, finely chopped
1 carrot, finely chopped
1 stalk celery, finely chopped
Pinch hot pepper flakes
2 mild or hot Italian sausages,
  casings removed (about 8 oz/
  250 g total)
2 plum tomatoes, diced

¼ cup (50 mL) chopped fresh basil
  or Italian parsley
¼ cup (50 mL) freshly grated
  Parmigiano-Reggiano or Romano
  cheese
¼ tsp (1 mL) salt
¼ tsp (1 mL) freshly ground black
  pepper
4 portobello mushrooms, stems
  removed

Makes 4 servings

With their natural cup, mushrooms are the perfect vehicle for stuffing. And portobello mushrooms are large and meaty enough to make a meal.

Tip

To lighten up the color of the mushroom and enhance the flavor, scoop out the gills with a small spoon before stuffing.

In a large skillet, heat oil over medium heat. Add garlic, onion, carrot, celery and hot pepper flakes; cook, stirring, for about 5 minutes or until softened. Add sausages and cook, breaking up with the back of a spoon, for about 8 minutes or until no longer pink. Add tomatoes; simmer, uncovered, for about 8 minutes or until slightly thickened. Stir in basil, cheese, salt and black pepper.

Divide mixture among mushrooms and place on a baking sheet lined with parchment paper. Bake in the center of a 375°F (190°C) oven for about 15 minutes or until mushrooms are tender. (*Let cool. Wrap in foil individually and reheat in 350°F/180°C oven for about 20 minutes or until hot.*)

VARIATION
Try using your favorite ground meat instead of sausage.

Per serving 310 calories, 14 g protein, 22 g fat, 13 g carbohydrates, 5 g fiber

Grilled Sausage on a Bun

Salsiccia Grigliata

Makes 4 servings

Here's a backyard and picnic favorite. Leftover sausages are delicious cold the next day.

Tip

You can vary the flavor of this treat by looking for turkey, veal, chicken or garlic sausages in local markets.

4 mild or hot Italian sausages (about 1 lb/500 g total)
2 tbsp (25 mL) extra-virgin olive oil
1 jar (12 oz/375 mL) mild or hot pickled vegetables, drained
¼ cup (50 mL) chopped tomatoes
2 tbsp (25 mL) chopped fresh Italian parsley
4 ciabatta or sausage buns

Slice sausages in half lengthwise almost all the way through, leaving them attached on one side. Place on a greased grill, over medium-high heat, and cook, brushing with oil and turning once, for about 12 minutes or until golden and crisp.

Meanwhile, finely chop vegetables and place in a small bowl. Add tomatoes and parsley and stir to combine. (*Cover and refrigerate for up to 8 hours.*)

Toast sausage buns in a 400°F (200°C) oven or on the grill. Place sausages in buns and top with vegetable mixture.

Per serving 440 calories, 19 g protein, 23 g fat, 38 g carbohydrates, 3 g fiber

Sausage, Peppers and Tomatoes

Salsiccia, Peperoni e Pomodori

2 tbsp (25 mL) extra-virgin olive oil
6 mild or hot Italian sausages
   (about 1½ lbs/750 g total)
5 cloves garlic, sliced
2 small red bell peppers, cut in
   thick slices
2 small yellow bell peppers, cut in
   thick slices

1 onion, sliced
10 fresh basil leaves, torn in half
1½ cups (375 mL) canned tomatoes,
   with juices, crushed with a fork
Pinch salt
Pinch freshly ground black pepper

Makes 6 servings

This recipe is from my dear friend Maria Marotta. Her family is from Puglia, a couple provinces over from Calabria, where my family is from. When we chat, we talk about family and food . . . and then more food. Maria serves this dish with rice or egg noodles, or just as is with warm homemade bread.

In a large ovenproof skillet or saucepan, heat oil over medium-high heat. Add sausages and brown on all sides. Using tongs, remove sausages to a plate.

To the oil remaining in the skillet, add garlic, red and yellow peppers and onion; cook, stirring, for 10 minutes or until golden. Add basil, tomatoes with juices, salt and black pepper; bring to a boil.

Meanwhile, slice sausages on the diagonal into 1-inch (2.5 cm) pieces. Add to skillet and cook for 5 minutes. Place skillet in the center of a 400°F (200°C) oven and roast for about 15 minutes or until sausage is no longer pink inside. *(Let cool. Cover and refrigerate for up to 1 day. Reheat in skillet over medium heat until hot.)*

Tip

When shopping for sausages, look for a pork and veal combination for a traditional Barese flavor.

Per serving 470 calories, 18 g protein, 40 g fat, 9 g carbohydrates, 2 g fiber

Roasted Sausages and Peppers

Salsiccia e Peperoni al Forno

Makes 6 servings

For me, this is pure comfort food. I love to cook these sausages for casual get-togethers, although I really don't need an excuse. My family adores them too. You can serve them with mustard, but it's more Italian to use a drizzle of pasta sauce.

Tip

Try other sausages, such as garlic, bratwurst, veal or turkey.

6 mild or hot Italian sausages (about 1½ lbs/750 g total)
1 tbsp (15 mL) extra-virgin olive oil
2 large red bell peppers, sliced
2 large green bell peppers, sliced

2 onions, sliced
Pinch salt
Pinch hot pepper flakes
6 panini or sausage buns

Using a small paring knife, cut shallow diagonal slashes across the sausages. Heat a nonstick skillet over medium-high heat. Add sausages and brown on all sides. Using tongs, transfer to an 11-x 7-inch (2 L) baking dish and set aside. Drain fat from skillet.

In the same skillet, heat oil over medium-high heat. Add red and green peppers, onions, salt and hot pepper flakes; cook, stirring constantly, for 3 minutes.

Spread pepper mixture evenly over sausages. Roast in the center of a 425°F (220°C) oven for about 25 minutes or until sausages are no longer pink inside. *(Cover and refrigerate for up to 2 days. Serve cold or reheat in microwave.)*

Place sausages in buns and top with pepper mixture.

Per serving 640 calories, 25 g protein, 40 g fat, 44 g carbohydrates, 5 g fiber

Sausage and Rice Chili

Chili di Salsiccia e Riso

3 mild Italian sausages, casings
  removed (about 12 oz/375 g total)
2 tsp (10 mL) extra-virgin olive oil
2 cloves garlic, minced
1 onion, chopped
2 tsp (10 mL) chili powder
1 tsp (5 mL) dried oregano
1½ cups (375 mL) Carnaroli or
  Arborio rice
2 cups (500 mL) pasta sauce (store-
  bought or see recipe, page 20)

2 cups (500 mL) chicken stock (store-
  bought or see recipe, page 22)
1 cup (250 mL) water
1 can (19 oz/540 mL) red kidney
  beans, drained and rinsed
1 green bell pepper, chopped
¼ tsp (1 mL) salt
¼ tsp (1 mL) freshly ground black
  pepper

Heat a large saucepan or Dutch oven over medium-high heat. Add sausage and cook, breaking up with the back of a spoon, for about 5 minutes or until no longer pink. Drain fat, if any.

Reduce heat to medium and add oil. Add garlic, onion, chili powder and oregano; cook, stirring, for about 5 minutes or until softened. Add rice and stir to coat. Add pasta sauce, stock and water; bring to a boil. Add beans, green pepper, salt and black pepper. Cover and simmer, stirring occasionally, for about 15 minutes or until rice is tender and chili has thickened.

VARIATION
Substitute 12 oz (375 g) lean ground beef, pork, turkey or chicken for the sausages.

Per each of 6 servings 510 calories, 21 g protein, 13 g fat, 78 g carbohydrates, 12 g fiber

Super-Fast Lasagna

Lasagna Rapida

Makes 4 servings

Wonton wrappers may not sound Italian, but many Italian restaurants use them to make ravioli and other stuffed pastas. They save a lot of time because you don't have to precook noodles. Just take the wrappers out of the package, and you're ready to go.

1½ cups (375 mL) chunky pasta
  sauce
⅓ cup (75 mL) water
1 pkg (8 oz/250 g) wonton wrappers
1 tub (16 oz/454 g) ricotta or puréed
  cottage cheese

1 cup (250 mL) finely chopped
  cooked mild or hot Italian sausage
Pinch freshly ground black pepper
2 cups (500 mL) shredded Italian
  cheese blend

In a small bowl, combine pasta sauce and water. Spread about ½ cup (125 mL) of the sauce in an 8-inch (2 L) baking dish. Cover bottom with wonton wrappers, overlapping slightly. Add another ⅓ cup (75 mL) of the sauce. Top with one third each of the ricotta and sausage. Sprinkle with pepper and ½ cup (125 mL) of the shredded cheese. Repeat layers two more times. Arrange the remaining wonton wrappers over top and spread with the remaining sauce and shredded cheese. *(Cover and refrigerate for up to 1 day.)*

Bake in a 350°F (180°C) oven for about 25 minutes or until bubbly. Let stand for 5 minutes before cutting.

Per serving 830 calories, 65 g protein, 42 g fat, 47 g carbohydrates, 2 g fiber

VARIATIONS

Substitute smoked turkey or ham or cooked ground beef for the sausage.

Instead of sausage, use 6 hard-cooked eggs, sliced.

WONTON RAVIOLI

Wonton wrappers are handy and easy to use in cooking and making ravioli without making homemade pasta.

Try easy fillings like the spinach and ricotta cannelloni filling in the wonton wrappers. Simply place a small amount in wrapper and fold over corner to corner. Dampen edges with water to help stick together.

For meat filling use the Bolognese sauce that has been chilled until firm.

You can make larger ravioli by using 2 wonton wrappers together to make squares.

Keep refrigerated until ready to use and boil in salted water until they float to the top. Toss with your favorite sauces such as pesto (see page 18) or butter sage sauce (page 68).

Tip

Italian cheese blend is a blend of 3 or 4 cheeses. It's available in the dairy aisle with other shredded cheeses.

beef

Italians don't use a lot of beef, but when they do, they try to use the best. My favorite cuts are sirloin and tenderloin; yes, they're a bit more expensive, but when cooked perfectly they're lean, meaty and juicy. Whether it's a roast or a pan-seared fillet, beef has a rich, melt-in-your-mouth texture that can't be beat. It's great for entertaining, but easy enough to prepare for a weeknight meal, perhaps for a special birthday or just to say I love you. (I usually say it with food!) On its own or served with potatoes or pasta, beef is tasty no matter how you slice it.

Ground beef is popular for family meals, as it's inexpensive and easy to cook. But that doesn't mean you have to make it the same way every time. Try new dishes, such as Family Mini Meatloaves (page 161) or Italian Meatball Subs (page 162).

Beef on the Run

Manzo alla Corsa

Makes 2 servings

This is a quick, flavorful way to prepare beef during the week. If you have some leftover sautéed mushrooms, add them to the sauce for a heartier flavor.

Tips

Some grocers sell beef already sliced; it is usually eye of the round.

For melt-in-your-mouth cutlets, thinly slice beef tenderloin yourself. You can also use eye of the round and thinly slice it.

1 tbsp (15 mL) extra-virgin olive oil	2 cups (500 mL) cherry tomatoes, halved
8 oz (250 g) beef tenderloin cutlets	2 tbsp (25 mL) red wine vinegar
¼ tsp (1 mL) freshly ground black pepper	½ cup (125 mL) halved pitted green olives
Pinch salt	2 tbsp (25 mL) chopped fresh Italian parsley
2 cloves garlic, minced	
1 onion, chopped	

In a nonstick skillet, heat oil over medium-high heat. Add beef and brown on both sides. Using tongs, remove beef to a plate and sprinkle with half each of the pepper and salt.

To the oil remaining in the skillet, add garlic and onion; reduce heat to medium and cook, stirring, for 5 minutes or until softened. Add tomatoes and the remaining pepper and salt; cook, stirring, for 5 minutes. Add vinegar and cook, stirring, for 1 minute. Return beef to sauce and add olives and parsley; stir to coat with sauce and cook until beef is heated through.

VARIATION
Substitute veal or pork cutlets for the beef.

Per serving 360 calories, 25 g protein, 23 g fat, 14 g carbohydrates, 3 g fiber

Beef Pizzaiola

Manzo alla Pizzaiola

1 lb (500 g) top sirloin grilling steak
1 tsp (5 mL) dried oregano
½ tsp (2 mL) salt
¼ tsp (1 mL) hot pepper flakes
1 tbsp (15 mL) extra-virgin olive oil
¼ cup (50 mL) dry white wine

4 cloves garlic, minced
2 anchovy fillets, minced
1 can (28 oz/796 mL) diced tomatoes
¼ cup (50 mL) chopped fresh Italian parsley
1 tbsp (15 mL) capers (optional)

Trim any visible fat from steak and slice thinly across the grain into 1-inch (2 cm) long pieces; place in a large bowl. Add half each of the oregano and salt and all of the hot pepper flakes; toss to coat. In a large nonstick skillet, heat oil over medium-high heat. Add beef, in batches if necessary, and brown on both sides. Transfer beef and juices to a bowl.

Add wine to the skillet and cook for 1 minute. Add garlic and anchovies; cook, stirring for about 1 minute or until turning golden. Add tomatoes, breaking up with the back of a spoon, and the remaining oregano and salt; bring to a boil. Reduce heat and boil gently, uncovered, for about 15 minutes or until thickened. Add beef and juices, parsley and capers, if using; cook until beef is heated through.

VARIATION
You can make this with chicken, veal, pork or even ground beef, or with veal cutlets or pork loin chops. For boneless skinless chicken breasts, cook in sauce for about 15 minutes or until no longer pink inside. For ground beef, brown, stirring, until fully cooked, then follow rest of recipe.

Per serving 330 calories, 29 g protein, 18 g fat, 12 g carbohydrates, 4 g fiber

Beef Tenderloin with Peppercorn Balsamic Drizzle

Manzo all'Aceto Balsamico e Pepe

Makes 8 servings

Lean and luscious, this roast will leave family and guests asking for more. Balsamic vinegar and mushrooms are one of the great Italian marriages. The ground dried porcini mushrooms make an earthy crust around this tender cut of beef, and the Peppercorn Balsamic Drizzle adds a spark of flavor. This is a special roast for a special occasion, but it's done in a snap.

Tip

Use a meat thermometer and insert it into the thickest part of the tenderloin. For medium rare, the meat thermometer should register 150°F (65°C); for medium, 160°F (70°C).

½ cup (125 mL) dried porcini mushrooms
1 tbsp (15 mL) peppercorns, crushed
1 tbsp (15 mL) coarse salt
1 beef tenderloin (about 2 lbs/500 g)
2 tbsp (25 mL) extra-virgin olive oil

Peppercorn Balsamic Drizzle
½ cup (125 mL) beef stock
½ cup (125 mL) balsamic vinegar
¼ cup (50 mL) water
2 tbsp (25 mL) packed brown sugar
1 tbsp (15 mL) mixed peppercorns

In a clean coffee grinder, grind porcini mushrooms to a fine powder. Place in a shallow dish and stir in peppercorns and salt.

Rub beef tenderloin with oil and coat evenly with mushroom mixture. Place in a small baking pan lined with foil. *(Cover and refrigerate for up to 4 hours.)*

Roast in a 500°F (260°C) oven for 15 minutes. Turn and roast for 10 minutes or until beef reaches an internal temperature of 140°F (60°C) for rare, or until desired doneness. Cover with foil and let stand for 5 minutes before slicing.

Peppercorn Balsamic Drizzle: Meanwhile, in a small saucepan, bring stock, vinegar, water, brown sugar and peppercorns to a boil over high heat. Reduce heat and simmer for about 10 minutes or until reduced by half. *(Cover and refrigerate for up to 8 hours. Reheat over low heat.)*

Strain Peppercorn Balsamic Drizzle into a serving dish and serve with beef.

Per serving 270 calories, 27 g protein, 13 g fat, 11 g carbohydrates, 2 g fiber

Family Mini Meatloaves

Minipolpettoni per la Famiglia

1 tbsp (15 mL) extra-virgin olive oil
2 cloves garlic, minced
1 small onion, chopped
½ red or green bell pepper, diced (optional)
1 tsp (5 mL) dried oregano
Pinch hot pepper flakes
1 egg, lightly beaten
¾ cup (175 mL) pasta or pizza sauce (store-bought or see recipe, page 20)

⅓ cup (75 mL) seasoned dry bread crumbs
¼ cup (50 mL) freshly grated Parmigiano-Reggiano cheese
½ tsp (2 mL) salt
¼ tsp (1 mL) freshly ground black pepper
1½ lbs (750 g) lean ground beef
½ cup (125 mL) shredded mozzarella cheese

Makes 12 mini meatloaves or 4 to 6 servings

I didn't grow up eating meatloaf, but times they are a-changing. These mini loaves are a big hit with kids and adults alike. My son Matthew (three years old) and cousin Alyssa (13 years old) agree— they are really good!

In a nonstick skillet, heat oil over medium heat. Add garlic, onion, red pepper (if using), oregano and hot pepper flakes; cook, stirring, for about 5 minutes or until softened. Let cool slightly.

Meanwhile, in a large bowl, combine egg, ¼ cup (50 mL) of the pasta sauce, bread crumbs, Parmigiano-Reggiano, salt and black pepper. Add beef and stir to combine. Add onion mixture and mix with your hands until well combined.

Divide among muffin tins. Top each with the remaining sauce and bake in the center of a 400°F (200°C) oven for 25 minutes. Sprinkle each with mozzarella and bake for 3 minutes or until cheese is melted and meat reaches an internal temperature of 160°F (75°C) and is no longer pink inside.

VARIATION
Substitute lean ground pork, veal or chicken for the beef. If using ground chicken, bake to an internal temperature of 175°F (80°C).

Per 1 mini meatloaf 180 calories, 14 g protein, 11 g fat, 5 g carbohydrates, 1 g fiber

Italian Meatball Subs

Panini al Polpette di Manzo

Makes 4 servings

Meatballs make versatile leftovers, great for take-away dinners or lunches. These are a family favorite—at least at my house!

1 egg
¼ cup (50 mL) seasoned dry bread
   crumbs
½ tsp (2 mL) freshly ground black
   pepper
¼ tsp (1 mL) salt
12 oz (375 g) lean ground beef

1 tbsp (15 mL) extra-virgin olive oil
1¼ cups (300 mL) pasta sauce (store-
   bought or see recipe, page 20)
4 sausage or submarine buns
½ cup (125 mL) shredded mozzarella
   cheese

In a medium bowl, whisk together egg, bread crumbs, pepper and salt. Add beef and mix with your hands until well combined. Shape into 1-inch (2.5 cm) balls, making about 20 meatballs.

In a large nonstick skillet, heat oil over medium-high heat. Add meatballs and cook, turning often, for about 10 minutes or until no longer pink inside. Drain off any fat. (*Cover and refrigerate for up to 2 days. Freeze for up to 1 month.*)

Pour pasta sauce over meatballs, stirring and scraping up any brown bits from bottom of skillet. Simmer, stirring occasionally, for about 5 minutes or until sauce is heated through.

Slice buns in half lengthwise. Divide meatballs and sauce evenly among the buns and sprinkle with cheese.

VARIATION
Substitute lean ground veal or pork for the beef.

Per serving 510 calories, 30 g protein, 22 g fat, 47 g carbohydrates, 4 g fiber

Bolognese Meat Sauce

Salsa Bolognese

1 tbsp (15 mL) extra-virgin olive oil
1 onion, finely chopped
1 small carrot, diced
1 stalk celery, diced
1 lb (500 g) lean ground beef
½ cup (125 mL) dry white wine
4 plum tomatoes, chopped
1 cup (250 mL) chicken stock (store-
   bought or see recipe, page 22)

¼ cup (50 mL) chopped fresh
   Italian parsley
½ tsp (2 mL) salt
Pinch freshly grated nutmeg
12 oz (375 g) fettuccine or linguine
⅓ cup (75 mL) freshly grated
   Parmigiano-Reggiano cheese

Makes 4 servings

This sauce can be cooked for up to 3 hours, but there's no need to do so if you're busy. It is thick and meaty enough to be enjoyed as a chili if you don't feel like pasta.

Tip
To save work, you can use 1 can (28 oz/796 mL) diced tomatoes for the plum tomatoes.

In a large saucepan, heat oil over medium heat. Add onion, carrot and celery; cook, stirring, for about 5 minutes or until softened. Increase heat to medium-high. Add beef and cook, stirring, for about 5 minutes or until no longer pink. Add wine and cook for 2 minutes or until evaporated. Add tomatoes, stock, half of the parsley, salt and nutmeg; bring to a boil. Reduce heat and boil gently, uncovered, for 10 minutes or until thickened. *(Cover and refrigerate for up to 2 days or freeze for up to 2 weeks. Thaw before using.)*

Meanwhile, in a large pot of boiling salted water cook fettuccine for about 10 minutes or until al dente (tender but firm to the bite). Drain, add to meat sauce and toss to coat. Sprinkle with cheese and the remaining parsley; toss to combine.

Per serving 580 calories, 37 g protein, 23 g fat, 57 g carbohydrates, 4 g fiber

Beef Strip Loin Pasta with Balsamic Cream

Manzo con Pasta e Panna all'Aceto Balsamico

Italians and Greeks are similar in that they enjoy eating and cooking. My first meeting with Executive Chef Tom Filippou from Upstairs at Loblaws Cooking Schools was one of intense culinary discussion: Should it be water or stock in the polenta? We eventually became good friends and colleagues. Tom has a flair for sauces, which is evident in this rich and luscious pasta dish. Whether he cooks Greek or Italian, all of his students (me included) fall in love with his culinary delights.

Balsamic Cream
1 tbsp (15 mL) butter
1 shallot, chopped
1 small clove garlic, minced
1 sprig fresh thyme (or ½ tsp/2 mL dried)
1 bay leaf
¾ cup (175 mL) balsamic vinegar
¼ cup (50 mL) dry white wine
1½ cups (375 mL) whipping (35%) cream
Pinch salt
Pinch freshly ground black pepper

1 lb (500 g) penne rigate or rotini
2 tbsp (25 mL) extra-virgin olive oil
4 oz (125 g) beef strip loin grilling steak, thinly sliced
2 portobello mushrooms, stemmed and thinly sliced
2 cloves garlic, minced
½ small yellow bell pepper, sliced
Pinch salt
Pinch freshly ground black pepper
2 plum tomatoes, diced
2 tbsp (25 mL) chopped fresh Italian parsley

Balsamic Cream: In a medium saucepan, melt butter over medium heat. Add shallot and garlic; cook, stirring, for about 3 minutes or until softened. Add thyme, bay leaf, balsamic vinegar and wine; boil gently, uncovered, for about 10 minutes or until reduced by half. Add whipping cream and boil gently for about 5 minutes or until sauce is thick enough to coat the back of a spoon. Remove sprig of thyme and bay leaf and add salt and pepper; keep warm. *(Cover and refrigerate for up to 4 hours. Reheat over low heat.)*

Meanwhile, in a large pot of boiling salted water, cook penne for about 10 minutes or until al dente (tender but firm to the bite). Drain and return to the pot.

In a large skillet, heat 1 tbsp (15 mL) of the oil over medium-high heat. Add beef and brown on both sides. Remove beef to a plate and keep warm.

Add the remaining oil, mushrooms, garlic, yellow pepper, salt and black pepper to the skillet; cook, stirring, for about 5 minutes or until mushrooms are golden brown. Add to pasta along with beef, tomatoes and Balsamic Cream; toss to coat. Transfer to a serving dish and sprinkle with parsley.

Per each of 6 servings 600 calories, 15 g protein, 33 g fat, 60 g carbohydrates, 4 g fiber

lamb
and veal

Many people save lamb for guests or special occasions, but is anything really too good for your family? Lamb is available fresh or frozen year-round, and with the many cuts now on the market it is easy to find one that suits your lifestyle. The leaner smaller cuts, such as racks and chops, are perfect for quick meals and make easy dinners for little hands. I enjoy picking up the chop bones; they're like chicken wings with class.

I make veal cutlets often—they're terrific for either dinner or lunch. Cold or hot, they are great on a ciabatta bun with a drizzle of leftover pasta sauce. You can always sneak one out of the fridge for a late-night snack or an early-morning breakfast.

Rack of Lamb with Fresh Herb and Garlic Crust

Carre d'Agnello con Aglio ed Erbe Aromatiche

Makes 2 to 4 servings

Quick enough for weeknights, but elegant enough for entertaining, here's a favorite with guests and family alike. The garlic in the crust marries perfectly with the rich lamb. Serve with roasted potatoes.

Tips

"Frenched" simply means that the rib bones are exposed and cleaned of fat. Ask the butcher to do this for you, if necessary.

For a different but equally delicious presentation, cut the rack into individual chops. Brown the chops, then sprinkle them with the bread crumb mixture and roast for about 8 minutes.

2 racks of lamb, frenched (about 1½ lbs/750 g total)	1 cup (250 mL) fresh bread crumbs
½ tsp (2 mL) freshly ground black pepper	2 tbsp (25 mL) shredded Asiago cheese
¼ tsp (1 mL) salt	2 tbsp (25 mL) chopped fresh Italian parsley
1 tbsp (15 mL) extra-virgin olive oil	2 tsp (10 mL) chopped fresh thyme
⅓ cup (75 mL) dry white wine	2 tsp (10 mL) chopped fresh rosemary
2 cloves garlic, minced	¼ cup (50 mL) butter, melted

Trim fat from lamb and sprinkle with half each of the pepper and salt. In a large nonstick skillet, heat oil over medium-high heat. Add lamb and brown well on both sides. Remove lamb to a small baking dish. Add wine to skillet and bring to a boil, stirring and scraping up any brown bits from bottom of skillet; pour over lamb.

In a small bowl, combine garlic, bread crumbs, cheese, parsley, thyme, rosemary and the remaining salt and pepper. Drizzle with butter and toss with a fork to coat. Pat bread crumb mixture onto lamb.

Roast in a 425°F (220°C) oven for about 15 minutes or until lamb reaches an internal temperature of 140°F (60°C) for rare, or until desired doneness.

Per each of 4 servings 500 calories, 24 g protein, 40 g fat, 8 g carbohydrates, 0 g fiber

Lamb with Artichokes

Agnello con Carciofi

2 racks of lamb, frenched (about
  1½ lbs/750 g total)
1 tbsp (15 mL) chopped fresh thyme
¼ tsp (1 mL) salt
¼ tsp (1 mL) freshly ground black
  pepper
1 tbsp (15 mL) extra-virgin olive oil

1 onion, thinly sliced
1 cup (250 mL) dry white wine
¼ cup (50 mL) butter
2 tbsp (25 mL) tomato paste
2 jars (each 6 oz/170 mL) marinated
  artichokes, drained
½ cup (125 mL) peas

Makes 4 to 6 servings

I enjoyed this dish
with veal chops on my
last night in Tuscany,
but it is exquisite with
lamb. Look for fresh
or frozen lamb year-
round to make this
dish for dinner or
special occasions.

Tips

If fresh thyme isn't available,
use 1 tsp (5 mL) dried.

On average, you will get
about 9 chops per rack of
lamb. You can also buy lamb
chops individually and serve
2 to 3 per person.

Slice lamb between bones into chops. Sprinkle evenly with thyme, salt and pepper. In a large deep nonstick skillet, heat oil over medium-high heat. Add lamb and brown on both sides. Using tongs, remove lamb to a plate and keep warm.

Add onion to the oil remaining in the skillet; cook, stirring, for about 8 minutes or until golden brown. Add wine and bring to a boil, stirring and scraping up any brown bits from bottom of skillet; boil for 2 minutes. Add butter and tomato paste; cook, stirring, for 1 minute. Add artichokes, peas and lamb; toss to coat with sauce. Reduce heat, cover and simmer for 5 minutes or until lamb chops are medium-rare, or until desired doneness.

Per each of 6 servings 400 calories, 17 g protein, 30 g fat, 9 g carbohydrates, 5 g fiber

Lamb Stew

Ragu d'Agnello

Makes 6 to 8 servings

The Irish are known for their lamb stew, but the Italian version is good too. Packed with tomatoes and artichokes, this stew is delicious served with rice or polenta to soak up the flavorful juices.

Tip

For a leaner, better-tasting stew, trim lamb of all visible fat.

2 tbsp (25 mL) extra-virgin olive oil	1 red bell pepper, chopped
2 lbs (1 kg) boneless leg of lamb, cut into ¾-inch (2 cm) pieces	1 jar (6 oz/170 g) marinated artichokes, drained
1 onion, chopped	1 can (28 oz/796 mL) tomatoes
1 carrot, chopped	1 cup (250 mL) beef stock
1 tsp (5 mL) dried thyme	Pinch salt
Pinch hot pepper flakes	Pinch freshly ground black pepper
½ cup (125 mL) dry white wine	

In a large shallow saucepan or Dutch oven, heat oil over medium-high heat. Add lamb, in batches, and brown on all sides. Using a slotted spoon or tongs, remove lamb to a plate.

To the oil remaining in the pan, add onion, carrot, thyme and hot pepper flakes; cook for 3 minutes or until onion is beginning to turn golden. Add wine and bring to a boil, stirring and scraping up any brown bits from bottom of skillet; boil for about 1 minute or until reduced by half. Add red pepper and artichokes; cook for 1 minute. Add lamb, tomatoes, stock, salt and black pepper; bring to a boil. Reduce heat and simmer, uncovered, for 35 minutes or until sauce is thickened and lamb is tender. *(Cover and refrigerate for up to 2 days or freeze for up to 2 weeks.)*

VARIATION

If you like, you can substitute beef for the lamb. I recommend using a top sirloin grilling steak.

Per each of 8 servings 300 calories, 23 g protein, 18 g fat, 10 g carbohydrates, 3 g fiber

Veal Piccata

Piccata di Vitello

⅓ cup (75 mL) all-purpose flour
¼ tsp (1 mL) salt
Pinch freshly ground black pepper
1 lb (500 g) thin-sliced veal cutlets
 (scaloppine)
3 tbsp (45 mL) butter
1 cup (250 mL) beef stock

3 tbsp (45 mL) chopped fresh Italian
 parsley
2 tbsp (25 mL) capers
½ tsp (2 mL) grated lemon rind
2 tbsp (25 mL) freshly squeezed
 lemon juice

Makes 4 servings

This tangy dish is so
quick and easy, you
may find yourself
making it more than
once a week. At my
house, we enjoy veal
two or three times a
week.

Tip
**This recipe is easy to double
for a larger crowd.**

In a shallow dish, combine flour, salt and pepper. Add veal and turn to coat evenly; shake off any excess. In a nonstick skillet, melt 2 tbsp (25 mL) of the butter over medium-high heat. Add veal, in batches, and cook, turning once, for about 5 minutes or until golden. Remove to a platter and keep warm.

Add stock to skillet and bring to a boil, stirring and scraping up any brown bits from bottom of skillet; boil for about 3 minutes or until reduced by half. Add parsley, capers, lemon rind and juice and the remaining butter; stir until butter is melted. Pour over veal cutlets.

VARIATION
For a change in flavor, substitute chicken, turkey or pork scaloppine. Cook until scaloppine are no longer pink inside.

Per serving 390 calories, 23 g protein, 29 g fat, 9 g carbohydrates, 1 g fiber

Veal Cutlets with Tomato Sauce

Cotolette di Vitello con Ragu di Pomodoro

Makes 4 servings

I love cutlets of all types and have included a number of recipes for them in this book. This one uses a quick method of breading. Leftover cutlets are great served in a bun for lunch the next day.

¼ cup (50 mL) all-purpose flour
½ tsp (2 mL) salt
½ tsp (2 mL) freshly ground
  black pepper
1 egg
3 tbsp (45 mL) water
¾ cup (175 mL) seasoned dry
  bread crumbs
¼ cup (50 mL) freshly grated
  Parmigiano-Reggiano or
  Romano cheese

1 tsp (5 mL) dried oregano
1 lb (500 g) thin-sliced veal cutlets
  (scaloppine)
¼ cup (50 mL) extra-virgin olive oil
  (approx)
4 cups (1 L) pasta sauce (store-
  bought or see recipe, page 20)

In a shallow dish, combine flour and half each of the salt and pepper. In another shallow dish, whisk egg with water. In a third shallow dish, combine bread crumbs, 2 tbsp (25 mL) of the cheese and oregano.

Sprinkle veal with the remaining salt and pepper. Add to flour mixture, turning to coat evenly, then dip in egg mixture, letting excess drip off. Add to bread crumb mixture and turn to coat evenly. Place on a baking sheet lined with waxed paper. *(Cover and refrigerate for up to 4 hours.)*

In a large nonstick skillet, heat oil over medium-high heat. Add veal, in batches, and cook, turning once, for about 4 minutes or until light golden, adding more oil as necessary.

Ladle some of the pasta sauce into a large shallow baking dish. Top with cutlets, overlapping slightly. Ladle the remaining sauce over top and sprinkle with the remaining cheese. Cover with foil and bake in a 350°F (180°C) oven for about 15 minutes or until sauce is bubbly and veal is no longer pink inside. *(Refrigerate for up to 1 day and reheat, covered, in 350°F/180°C oven for about 25 minutes or until hot.)*

Tip

These cutlets are also delicious without the sauce. Enjoy them right out of the skillet with some rapini or another favorite vegetable on the side.

Per serving 700 calories, 31 g protein, 44 g fat, 46 g carbohydrates, 7 g fiber

Veal Cutlets with Garlic Mushrooms and Peppers

Cotolette di Vitello con Funghi all'Aglio e Peperoni

Makes 4 servings

I love cutlets of all types and have included a number of recipes for them in this book. This one uses a quick method of breading. Leftover cutlets are great served in a bun for lunch the next day.

Tip
Substitute pounded boneless skinless chicken breasts or pork schnitzel for the veal. Cook until cutlets are no longer pink.

1 cup (250 mL) seasoned dry
  bread crumbs
2 tbsp (25 mL) freshly grated
  Parmigiano-Reggiano cheese
1 tsp (5 mL) dried oregano
Pinch salt
Pinch freshly ground black pepper
1 lb (500 g) thin-sliced veal cutlets
  (scaloppine)
¼ cup (50 mL) extra-virgin olive oil

Garlic Mushrooms and Peppers
2 tbsp (25 mL) extra-virgin olive oil
4 cloves garlic, minced
1 onion, sliced
12 oz (375 g) mushrooms, sliced
Pinch hot pepper flakes
1 red bell pepper, chopped
1 green bell pepper, chopped
¼ cup (50 mL) pasta sauce (store-
  bought or see recipe, page 20)
¼ tsp (1 mL) salt
¼ tsp (1 mL) freshly ground black
  pepper

In a shallow dish, combine bread crumbs, cheese, oregano, salt and pepper. Add veal and turn to coat evenly. In a large nonstick skillet, heat oil over medium-high heat. Add veal, in batches, and cook, turning once, for about 8 minutes or until golden brown. Remove to a plate and keep warm.

Garlic Mushrooms and Peppers: Meanwhile, in another skillet, heat oil over medium-high heat. Add garlic, onion, mushrooms and hot pepper flakes; cook, stirring, for about 10 minutes or until no liquid remains and mushrooms are browned. Add red and green peppers; cook for 5 minutes or until peppers are starting to soften. Stir in pasta sauce and cook for 2 minutes or until heated through. Add salt and black pepper and serve with cutlets.

Per serving 600 calories, 30 g protein, 40 g fat, 31 g carbohydrates, 5 g fiber

Veal Chops with Mushrooms and Peppers

Vitello con Funghi e Peperoni

2 tsp (10 mL) dried oregano
1 tsp (5 mL) dried basil
½ tsp (2 mL) salt
½ tsp (2 mL) freshly ground black
  pepper
4 veal loin chops, trimmed (about
  1¼ lbs/625 g total)
1 tbsp (15 mL) extra-virgin olive oil
4 cloves garlic, minced

1 onion, chopped
1 red bell pepper, chopped
8 oz (250 g) mushrooms, sliced
2 tbsp (25 mL) all-purpose flour
1½ cups (375 mL) chicken stock
  (store-bought or see recipe, page 22)
2 tbsp (25 mL) chopped fresh Italian
  parsley

Makes 4 servings

Veal chops are lean and cook quickly enough for weeknight meals. This one-pan dinner is easy to make and has a delicious garlicky sauce. Serve with egg noodles or pasta.

In a small bowl, combine oregano, basil, salt and black pepper. Sprinkle veal evenly with half of the mixture.

In a large nonstick skillet, heat oil over medium-high heat. Add veal and cook, turning once, for 5 minutes or until golden brown. Using tongs, remove veal to a plate.

To the oil remaining in the skillet, add garlic, onion, red pepper, mushrooms and the remaining herb mixture; cook, stirring, for about 8 minutes or until no liquid remains and vegetables are softened. Sprinkle with flour and cook, stirring, for 30 seconds. Add stock and bring to a boil, stirring and scraping up any brown bits. Cook, stirring, for 2 minutes or until thickened; add parsley. Return veal to skillet and turn to coat. Reduce heat, and simmer for 5 minutes or until just a hint of pink remains inside veal.

Per serving 320 calories, 28 g protein, 18 g fat, 12 g carbohydrates, 2 g fiber

Nana Ortenzia's Meatballs

Polpette di Nana Ortenzia

1 egg
1 clove garlic, minced
½ cup (125 mL) fresh bread crumbs
2 tbsp (25 mL) finely chopped fresh Italian parsley
2 tbsp (25 mL) freshly grated Parmigiano-Reggiano cheese
½ tsp (2 mL) salt
Pinch hot pepper flakes
8 oz (250 g) ground veal
8 oz (250 g) ground pork
3 cups (750 mL) pasta sauce (store-bought or see recipe, page 20)

In a large bowl, whisk together egg, garlic, bread crumbs, parsley, cheese, salt and hot pepper flakes. Add veal and pork; mix with your hands until well combined. Shape into 1-inch (2.5 cm) balls, making about 24 meatballs. Place on a baking sheet lined with foil.

Bake in a 350°F (180°C) oven for about 12 minutes or until no longer pink inside, but not browned. *(Let cool completely. Place in airtight container and refrigerate for up to 2 days or freeze up to 1 month.)*

Meanwhile, in a large saucepan, heat pasta sauce over medium heat. Add meatballs and boil gently, uncovered, for about 10 minutes for flavors to blend.

Per each of 6 servings 270 calories, 18 g protein, 15 g fat, 15 g carbohydrates, 3 g fiber

Veal-Stuffed Peppers

Peperoni Ripieni di Vitello

1 tbsp (15 mL) extra-virgin olive oil
2 anchovy fillets, finely chopped
1 onion, chopped
8 oz (250 g) lean ground veal
Pinch salt
Pinch freshly ground black pepper
2 eggs, lightly beaten
¾ cup (175 mL) fresh bread crumbs

1 cup (250 mL) ricotta cheese
½ cup (125 mL) shredded Asiago
  cheese
¼ cup (50 mL) chopped fresh Italian
  parsley
2 tbsp (25 mL) capers
4 red or orange bell peppers

Makes 4 to 6 servings

I love stuffed peppers, and for many years made the tried-and-true version with rice and ground beef. Then I experimented and found that ground veal is equally delicious. Here, it works as a good foil to the sharp flavors in the stuffing.

Tips

See page 4 for instructions on making fresh bread crumbs. For added flavor, toast them in a skillet with some oil and garlic.

I like my peppers slightly crisp, not completely soft. For a softer pepper, increase the total baking time to about 55 minutes, baking uncovered for the last 10 minutes.

In a large nonstick skillet, heat oil over medium heat. Add anchovies and onion; cook, stirring, for 3 minutes or until onion is softened. Add veal, salt and black pepper; cook for about 5 minutes or until no longer pink. Scrape into a large bowl and add eggs, bread crumbs, ricotta, Asiago, parsley and capers; mix to combine well.

Cut peppers in half lengthwise and remove ribs and seeds. Stuff with filling and place in a 13- x 9-inch (3 L) greased baking dish. Cover with foil. (*Refrigerate for up to 1 day. Add about 10 minutes to the baking time.*)

Bake in the center of a 400°F (200°C) oven for 30 minutes. Remove foil and bake for 10 minutes or until peppers are tender-crisp and filling is light golden.

VARIATION
Substitute lean ground pork for the veal.

Per each of 6 servings 260 calories, 19 g protein, 15 g fat, 13 g carbohydrates, 2 g fiber

fish and seafood

Fish has so many health benefits, it's no wonder so many people are eating more of it. But don't forget that it tastes great too. Fillets of salmon and tilapia are popular at my house, and I'm delighted when my small son asks for salmon for dinner.

Whether you catch the fish yourself or buy it at the market, you will love the recipes in this chapter. Simple to prepare, but full of flavors such as fresh herbs and tomatoes, these dishes will make you want to cook fish more than once a week.

Shrimp, mussels, clams and scallops are all great additions to weeknight meals. You can keep a bag of shrimp or scallops in the freezer and be ready for uninvited guests or to whip up something a little extra-special for Friday night dinner.

Salmon Fillets with Wine

Filetti di Salmone al Vino

Makes 4 servings

White wine enhances many dishes, and here it creates a flavorful sauce to cook the salmon in. Paired with rice, this makes a quick, elegant meal.

1 tbsp (15 mL) extra-virgin olive oil
6 plum tomatoes, chopped
4 fresh basil leaves
2 cloves garlic, smashed
1 sprig fresh thyme
⅓ cup (75 mL) dry white wine

Pinch salt
Pinch freshly ground black pepper
4 salmon fillets, skin removed (each about 6 oz/175 g)
1 tbsp (15 mL) chopped fresh Italian parsley

In a large shallow saucepan, heat oil over medium heat. Add tomatoes and cook for 5 minutes or until starting to become soft. Add basil, garlic, thyme and wine; bring to a boil. Reduce heat and simmer, uncovered, for 10 minutes. Add salt and pepper.

Add salmon to tomato mixture; cover and cook for 5 minutes. Turn fillets, cover and cook for about 3 minutes or until fish is opaque and flakes easily when tested with a fork. Sprinkle with parsley.

Per serving 340 calories, 37 g protein, 18 g fat, 5 g carbohydrates, 1 g fiber

Prosciutto-Wrapped Salmon

Salmone col Prosciutto

3 tbsp (45 mL) chopped fresh Italian
  parsley
2 tbsp (25 mL) chopped fresh basil
1 tbsp (15 mL) chopped fresh thyme
¼ tsp (1 mL) freshly ground black
  pepper

Pinch salt
1 tbsp (15 mL) extra-virgin olive oil
4 wild or Atlantic salmon fillets, skin
  removed (each about 6 oz/175 g)
12 thin slices prosciutto

Makes 4 servings

Thin, salty slices of prosciutto wrap rich, hearty salmon fillets for a simple but lovely presentation. Guests don't need to know this dish took you next to no time to put together!

In a small bowl, combine parsley, basil, thyme, pepper and salt. Rub salmon with oil and sprinkle evenly with herb mixture. Wrap each fillet completely with 3 slices of prosciutto and place on a baking sheet lined with parchment paper.

Roast in a 425°F (220°C) oven for about 15 minutes or until fish is opaque and flakes easily when tested with a fork and prosciutto is golden brown.

VARIATIONS

Try wrapping scallops and shrimp with prosciutto. Roast in oven for about 8 minutes. Can also be used as an appetizer.

If fresh herbs are not available, substitute 2 tsp (10 mL) dried basil and 1 tsp (5 mL) dried thyme.

Per serving 390 calories, 44 g protein, 24 g fat, 0.5 g carbohydrates, 0 g fiber

Fried Fish

Pesce Fritto

Makes 6 servings

I am a huge fan of battered fish, but it can sometimes feel heavy. A lighter batter such as this one solves the problem. My mom uses this batter to coat fish, shrimp and calamari. The results are crisp, golden and not at all heavy.

Tip

If your deep-fryer doesn't have a temperature gauge, use a deep-fat (candy) thermometer to make sure the oil stays at the right temperature as you cook.

6 cups (1.5 L) vegetable oil
1 cup (250 mL) all-purpose flour
1 cup (250 mL) water
2 tsp (10 mL) baking powder
½ tsp (2 mL) salt

2 lbs (1 kg) fish fillets (such as tilapia or haddock), cut into 4-inch (10 cm) pieces
6 lemon wedges

In a deep-fryer or a large heavy saucepan, heat oil to 375°F (190°C) over medium heat.

In a medium bowl, whisk together flour, water, baking powder and salt until smooth. Dip fish fillets in batter, letting excess drip off.

Gently place 1 fillet at a time in hot oil and fry, turning once, for about 5 minutes or until golden. Using a slotted spoon, remove to a plate lined with paper towels. Repeat with remaining fillets. Serve immediately with lemon wedges.

Per serving 280 calories, 25 g protein, 16 g fat, 10 g carbohydrates, 0 g fiber

Pan-Fried Tilapia with Caper Wine Sauce

1 egg
2 tbsp (25 mL) water
1/3 cup (75 mL) all purpose flour
1/4 tsp (1 mL) salt
1/4 tsp (1 mL) freshly ground black
  pepper
Pinch dried oregano
4 tilapia fillets (about 1 1/2 lbs/750 g
  total)
1/4 cup (50 mL) extra-virgin olive oil

Caper Wine Sauce
1 tbsp (15 mL) extra-virgin olive oil
2 cloves garlic, minced
1 small onion, finely chopped
1/3 cup (75 mL) dry white wine
1 tbsp (15 mL) capers
2 tbsp (25 mL) chopped fresh Italian
  parsley
2 tbsp (25 mL) freshly squeezed
  lemon juice
Pinch freshly ground black pepper

Makes 4 servings

Pan-fried fish is a quick and easy weeknight meal. The tilapia is delectable, but you can also use other favorite fillets, such as catfish or haddock. Serve with sautéed rapini and rice.

Pesce Fritto con Caperi e Vino

In a shallow dish, whisk together egg and water. In another shallow dish, combine flour, salt, pepper and oregano. Pat tilapia fillets with a paper towel and dip in egg mixture, letting excess drip off. Add to flour mixture and turn to coat evenly.

In a large nonstick skillet, heat oil over medium-high heat. Add fillets and cook, turning once, for about 8 minutes or until fish is golden brown and flakes easily when tested with a fork. Remove to a platter.

Per serving 400 calories, 29 g protein, 26 g fat, 10 g carbohydrates, 1 g fiber

Halibut Steaks with Pesto Topping

Pesce al Pesto

This is so easy it's almost embarrassing when people ask for the recipe! It's just fish and pesto, but it has gorgeous flavor that matches up perfectly with buttered pasta or long-grain rice.

4 halibut steaks, ½-inch (1 cm) thick (about 1½ lbs/750 g total)
¼ cup (50 mL) light mayonnaise
3 tbsp (45 mL) pesto (store-bought or see recipe, page 18)

1 tbsp (15 mL) finely chopped pitted black olives
1 tbsp (15 mL) freshly grated Parmigiano-Reggiano cheese
Pinch freshly ground black pepper

Place halibut on a baking sheet lined with parchment paper.

In a small bowl, whisk together mayonnaise, pesto, olives, cheese and pepper. Spread evenly over halibut.

Roast in a 425°F (220°C) oven for about 10 minutes or until fish is opaque and flakes easily when tested with a fork.

Per serving 400 calories, 25 g protein, 32 g fat, 2 g carbohydrates, 1 g fiber

Stuffed Fish Rolls

Braciole di Pesce

1¾ lbs (875 g) marlin or swordfish
  steak
1 whole egg
1 egg yolk
1 small clove garlic, minced
1 cup (250 mL) fresh bread crumbs
½ cup (125 mL) finely diced Asiago or
  provolone piccante cheese
2 tbsp (25 mL) finely chopped shallot
2 tbsp (25 mL) chopped fresh Italian
  parsley

2 tbsp (25 mL) chopped fresh basil
1 tbsp (15 mL) capers
Pinch hot pepper flakes
Pinch salt
Pinch freshly ground black pepper
1 tbsp (15 mL) extra-virgin olive oil
½ cup (125 mL) fish or chicken stock
  (store-bought or see recipe, page 22)
Lemon wedges

Makes 6 to 8 servings

These shark fillets are stuffed with a smooth, spicy and cheesy filling. My mother found these so unique and tender (she was the one who suggested this creation) that she started eating them cold out of the fridge! I quickly followed her lead—they were addictive! Rice or a green salad would be a perfect match alongside.

Tip

See page 4 for instructions on making fresh bread crumbs.

Slice about 1½ lbs (750 g) of the marlin steak into 16 thin slices; set aside.

Finely chop the remaining marlin and place in a medium bowl. Add whole egg, egg yolk, garlic, bread crumbs, cheese, shallot, parsley, basil, capers and hot pepper flakes; stir until combined.

Lay fish slices out on a work surface. Place 1 mounded tbsp (15 mL) fish mixture in the center of each slice and roll up. Sprinkle with salt and pepper.

In a large nonstick skillet, heat oil over medium-high heat. Add fish rolls seam side down, in batches if necessary, and cook about 3 minutes or until light golden on one side. Turn and add stock. Bring to a boil, cover and steam for 5 minutes or until fish is opaque and cheese melts inside. Serve with lemon wedges.

Per each of 8 servings 170 calories, 18 g protein, 8 g fat, 5 g carbohydrates, 0 g fiber

Cod with Tomatoes and Potatoes

Baccala con Pomodori e Patate

Makes 4 servings

This dish is a staple during the holidays, or on Fridays, when fish is traditionally eaten. My grandfather loved cod, and my grandmother would make some kind of fish dish every Friday.

2 Yukon gold potatoes, peeled and thinly sliced (about 6 oz/175 g total)	1 can (28 oz/796 mL) diced tomatoes
2 tbsp (25 mL) extra-virgin olive oil	1 bay leaf
2 green onions, chopped	½ tsp (2 mL) salt
2 cloves garlic, minced	½ tsp (2 mL) freshly ground black pepper
1 leek (white and light green parts only), thinly sliced	1 lb (500 g) cod fillets

Place potatoes in a small saucepan and cover with water; cover and bring to a boil over high heat. Boil for 5 minutes, drain well and set aside.

Meanwhile, in a large saucepan, heat oil over medium heat. Add green onions, garlic and leek; cook, stirring, for about 8 minutes or until softened. Add tomatoes, bay leaf, salt and pepper; bring to a boil. Add potatoes, cover and boil gently for 15 minutes or until slightly thickened. Gently stir in cod and cook, uncovered, for about 8 minutes or until fish is opaque and flakes easily when tested with a fork.

Per serving 250 calories, 16 g protein, 8 g fat, 29 g carbohydrates, 5 g fiber

Fried Cod with Onions

Baccala Fritto con Cipolle

1 tbsp (15 mL) extra-virgin olive oil
2 onions, thinly sliced
2 cloves garlic, minced
2 tbsp (25 mL) balsamic vinegar
6 cups (1.5 L) vegetable oil
½ cup (125 mL) all-purpose flour
½ cup (125 mL) water

1 tbsp (15 mL) finely chopped
 Italian parsley
1 tsp (5 mL) baking powder
½ tsp (2 mL) grated lemon rind
Pinch salt
Pinch freshly ground black pepper
1 lb (500 g) cod fillets, cut in 3-inch
 (8 cm) pieces

In a nonstick skillet, heat olive oil over medium-high heat. Add onions and garlic; cook, stirring, for about 5 minutes or until golden. Reduce heat to medium-low and cook, stirring occasionally, for 10 minutes or until softened and golden brown. Stir in balsamic vinegar; set aside.

Meanwhile, in a deep-fryer or a large heavy saucepan, heat vegetable oil to 375°F (190°C) over medium heat.

In a small bowl, whisk together flour, water, parsley, baking powder, lemon rind, salt and pepper until smooth. Dip cod fillets in batter, letting excess drip off.

Gently place 2 fillets at a time in hot oil and fry, turning once, for about 5 minutes or until golden. Using a slotted spoon, remove to a plate lined with paper towels. Repeat with remaining fillets.

Transfer fish to a serving platter and top with onion mixture.

Per serving 220 calories, 17 g protein, 11 g fat, 13 g carbohydrates, 1 g fiber

Sweet-and-Sour Red Snapper

Pesce Agrodolce

Makes 6 servings

Michael Mandato is the executive chef at Fairmont Jasper Park Lodge, which I've had the pleasure of visiting for the last six years for "Christmas in November," a fairy-tale event for holiday lovers. Michael shared this recipe with me as he shared his Southern Italian family stories . The sweet honey and peppers and the sour vinegar create the perfect balance of flavors in this tasty sauce.

Tips

For a richer flavor, Michael pan-fries the fillets in both butter and oil. You can too: use half butter and half oil.

I use my potato masher to crush the plum tomatoes in a shallow bowl.

¼ cup (50 mL) extra-virgin olive oil
2 cloves garlic, minced
1 large onion, thinly sliced
1 large red bell pepper, sliced
1 can (28 oz/796 mL) tomatoes, crushed
¼ cup (50 mL) red wine vinegar
¼ cup (50 mL) liquid honey
1 tbsp (15 mL) fancy molasses
1 tbsp (15 mL) Worcestershire sauce
¼ tsp (1 mL) hot pepper flakes
1 tbsp (15 mL) chopped fresh coriander or Italian parsley
1 tbsp (15 mL) chopped fresh basil
6 red snapper, perch or tilapia fillets (each about 6 oz/175 g)
¼ tsp (1 mL) salt
¼ tsp (1 mL) freshly ground black pepper

In a large skillet, heat 2 tbsp (25 mL) of the oil over medium heat. Add garlic, onion and red pepper; cook, stirring, for about 5 minutes or until softened. Add tomatoes, vinegar, honey, molasses, Worcestershire sauce and hot pepper flakes; bring to a boil. Reduce heat and simmer, uncovered, for about 25 minutes or until thickened. Stir in coriander and basil.

Meanwhile, sprinkle snapper evenly with salt and black pepper. In a nonstick skillet, heat the remaining oil over medium-high heat. Add snapper and cook, turning once, for about 8 minutes or until golden brown. Serve topped with sauce.

AGRODOLCE

Agrodolce is a classic sweet-and-sour Italian dish (dolce means "sweet" and agro means "sour").

Per serving 290 calories, 25 g protein, 10 g fat, 25 g carbohydrates, 2 g fiber

Mixed Fish Stew

Zuppa di Pesce

2 tbsp (25 mL) extra-virgin olive oil
4 cloves garlic, minced
1 onion, chopped
1 green bell pepper, chopped
1 can (28 oz/796 mL) diced tomatoes
1 cup (250 mL) fish or chicken stock
 (store-bought or see recipe, page 22)
½ cup (125 mL) chopped fresh Italian
 parsley

½ cup (125 mL) dry red wine
2 tbsp (25 mL) chopped fresh basil
 (or ½ tsp/2 mL dried)
1 tsp (5 mL) dried oregano
½ tsp (2 mL) hot pepper flakes
1 lb (500 g) mussels, rinsed
8 oz (250 g) cod fillets
8 oz (250 g) large shrimp, peeled
 and deveined

Makes 3 servings

This Italian-influenced fish stew is similar to bouillabaisse. The combination of fish and shellfish makes it an elegant dish for entertaining.

Tips

Try to get the freshest fish and seafood available. They will taste of the sea and won't have a fishy aroma. Ask your fishmonger when deliveries come in.

Check mussels before cooking. The shells should be tightly closed. If a shell is slightly open, give it a little tap; if it doesn't close, discard it. Once they are cooked, discard any that have not opened.

In a large saucepan, heat oil over medium heat. Add garlic, onion and green pepper; cook, stirring, for about 5 minutes or until softened. Add tomatoes, stock, half of the parsley, the wine, basil, oregano and hot pepper flakes; bring to a boil. Reduce heat and simmer, uncovered, for 15 minutes.

Add mussels, cod and shrimp; cover and simmer for about 10 minutes or until mussels open, cod is opaque and shrimp are pink and opaque. Gently stir in the remaining parsley.

Per serving 390 calories, 37 g protein, 13 g fat, 26 g carbohydrates, 7 g fiber

Pasta with Clams and Ricotta

Pasta con Vongole e Ricotta

Makes 4 servings

Some people say you should never combine cheese and fish, but you can break the rules—it's your kitchen!

Tips

For a spicier sauce, increase the hot pepper flakes to ½ tsp (2 mL).

You can use fresh clams instead of canned. Rinse them well to remove any grit and cook in sauce until they open.

2 tbsp (25 mL) extra-virgin olive oil
2 cloves garlic, minced
1 tsp (5 mL) dried oregano
¼ tsp (1 mL) hot pepper flakes
1 can (10 oz/284 g) clams, drained and rinsed
1 can (28 oz/796 mL) diced tomatoes
¼ tsp (1 mL) salt
¼ tsp (1 mL) freshly ground black pepper
1 lb (500 g) tagliatelle or fettuccine
1 egg
1 cup (250 mL) ricotta cheese
¼ cup (50 mL) freshly grated Parmigiano-Reggiano cheese
2 tbsp (25 mL) chopped fresh Italian parsley

In a large nonstick skillet, heat oil over medium heat. Add garlic, oregano and hot pepper flakes; cook, stirring, for 1 minute. Add clams and cook, stirring, for 3 minutes. Add tomatoes, salt and black pepper; reduce heat and simmer, uncovered, for 15 minutes.

Meanwhile, in a large pot of boiling salted water, cook pasta for 8 to 10 minutes or until al dente (tender but firm to the bite). Drain and return to the pot.

In a small bowl, whisk together egg, ricotta, Parmigiano-Reggiano and parsley. Toss with pasta to coat and divide onto plates. Ladle tomato clam sauce over top.

VARIATION
This dish is also delicious with mussels or small shrimp. Reduce cooking time to 10 minutes.

Per serving 660 calories, 37 g protein, 21 g fat, 80 g carbohydrates, 7 g fiber

Index